Introducing Vy

Sandra Smidt takes the reader on a journey through the key concepts of Lev Vygotsky, one of the twentieth century's most influential theorists in the field of early education. His ground-breaking principles of early learning and teaching are unpicked here using everyday language, and critical links between his fascinating ideas are revealed.

Introducing Vygotsky is an invaluable companion for anyone involved with children in the early years. The introduction of Vygotsky's key concepts is followed by discussion of the implications of these for teaching and learning. Each chapter also includes a useful glossary of terms.

This accessible text is illustrated throughout with examples drawn from real-life early years settings and the concepts discussed include:

- mediation and memory,
- culture and cultural tools,
- mental functions,
- language, concepts and thinking,
- activity theory,
- play and meaning.

This book is an inspiring reminder that learning is something that happens all the time, through the interactions learners have with more experienced 'others' who may be either adults or children.

Essential reading for all those interested in or working with children, *Introducing Vygotsky* emphasises the social nature of learning and examines the importance of issues such as culture, history, language and symbols in learning.

Sandra Smidt is a writer and consultant in early years education.

Introducing Vygotsky

A guide for practitioners and students in early years education

Sandra Smidt

LONDON AND NEW YORK

First published 2009
by Routledge
2 Park Square, Milton Park, Abingdon, Oxon OX14 4RN

Simultaneously published in the USA and Canada
by Routledge
270 Madison Avenue, New York, NY 10016

Reprinted 2009

Routledge is an imprint of the Taylor & Francis Group, an informa business

© 2009 Sandra Smidt

Typeset in Garamond and Gill by
Bookcraft Ltd, Stroud, Gloucestershire

Printed and bound in Great Britain by
CPI Antony Rowe, Chippenham, Wiltshire

All rights reserved. No part of this book may be reprinted
or reproduced or utilised in any form or by any electronic,
mechanical, or other means, now known or hereafter invented,
including photocopying and recording, or in any information
storage or retrieval system, without permission in writing from
the publishers.

British Library Cataloguing in Publication Data
A catalogue record for this book is available from the British
Library

Library of Congress Cataloging in Publication Data
Smidt, Sandra, 1943–
Introducing Vygotsky : a guide for practitioners and students in
early years education / Sandra Smidt.—1st ed.
 p. cm.
 Includes bibliographical references and index.
 1. Vygotskii, L. S. (Lev Semenovich), 1896–1934. 2. Early childhood education. 3. Child development—Social aspects. I. Title.
LB775.V942S65 2008
372.21—dc22   2008029006

ISBN10: 0-415-48055-8 (hbk)
ISBN10: 0-415-48057-4 (pbk)

ISBN13: 978-0-415-48055-0 (hbk)
ISBN13: 978-0-415-48057-4 (pbk)

My thanks to the children whose voices appear in this book, and to their parents and carers and educators who noticed and respected what they said and did enough to observe it, talk about it and sometimes record and analyse it.

My thanks, too, to my friend Hazel Abel whose enthusiasm for my proposal to write this book kept me on-task and who volunteered for the thankless job of reading it in draft.

Contents

List of figures viii
Preface ix

Introduction 1

1 Beginnings: towards a sociohistorical appreciation 7

2 On mediation, memory and cultural tools 21

3 More on culture, context and tools 41

4 On language, concepts and thinking 58

5 Learning and teaching 73

6 Activity theory 90

7 On play and meaning 103

8 On bridging the gap: more about the ZPD 121

9 What we have learned: a summary 139

10 Vygotsky's children 157

A final word 167

Bibliography 169
Index 175

Figures

2.1	The experience of the world that children have mediated by adults or more expert others	25
2.2	The experiences of the world that more expert others have mediated by text or other cultural tools	26
2.3	The goal of instruction – in this case the child's experience of the world mediated by text or other cultural tools	26
2.4	Child with more expert other using text to mediate experience	26
2.5	Hannah's labels	32
3.1	Bronfenbrenner's ecological model	45
4.1	Ben's figure, with onion-skin plaster cast and toothpick crutch	68
6.1	The first generation of activity theory	91
6.2	Second-generation activity theory model	91
7.1	Assisting a child through the zone of proximal development	118
10.1	The possible effects and combinations of the two axes of natural and cultural	160

Preface

This book has been written particularly for the many people who work with or care for young children and find it difficult to understand the work of one of the most important theorists in the field of early education – that of the great Russian thinker Lev Vygotsky. His work is difficult to understand partly because we only have access to it in translation and partly because it is full of wonderful ideas and theories which are difficult to unpack because they are written in dense and academic language. More than that, even those who have written about his work tend to keep to that academic language, which often means that the lay reader has to keep referring back to a dictionary. This makes the reading slow and laborious and, in my experience, many readers just give up. In writing this 'beginner's guide' I have often found myself trying to find a way into explaining something which is difficult to understand using everyday language. But – just like a young child – my interest in the subject and my great admiration for Vygotsky have kept me on-task, and I find myself now more able to think about the work of Vygotsky without continually having to refer to a text. In trying to 'teach' you about his work I have become aware of my own knowledge of the subject and have started to be able to think more abstractly. Much of what we say about young learners applies to learning throughout life. Tackling something new successfully often depends on previous experience and access to useful cultural tools. At the end of this book I hope you will understand this.

The book looks at some of the key themes in the work of Vygotsky, particularly those that apply to learning and to teaching. You will notice some words or phrases in italic script. These are key words or ideas and you may find the individual words in the glossary at the end of each chapter. Here the words are explained and their relevance to teaching and learning indicated. Each chapter ends with a brief closing section called 'Looking back, looking ahead'. This summarises what has been covered in the chapter and explains what will be dealt with in the next chapter. This is a technique to allow you to both reflect on what you have read and think about what is coming.

For me, writing this book has been a challenging, involving and satisfying task. It has been challenging because making the incomprehensible comprehensible, which is part of what I set out to do, is difficult and really requires whoever is doing this to really understand each point made. I have become my own teacher and have had to become aware of what I know and what I need to know better. So I have developed metacognitive skills. It has been involving because the more I have read the more links I have found. I didn't start off thinking about the work of people like Paolo Freire or Augusto Boal in terms of Vygotsky, but precisely because they were all concerned with learning as a social and liberating force this link emerged. And it has been satisfying because considering and making the links has made me realise just how much influence Vygotsky had and will have on education. I hope you enjoy reading this as much as I have enjoyed writing it.

Sandra Smidt
March 2008

Introduction

Setting the scene: a developmental diary

When my own children were born I was too young, too ignorant, too nervous and definitely too tired to do anything other than love them and care for them. They seemed just babies to me. But when my first grandchild was born I had developed an intense interest in and knowledge of early learning and development. So I watched this little baby and kept a very primitive sort of developmental diary, based on photographs I took of her and observations I made. At the time I did not know that such legendary figures as Charles Darwin, among others, had kept diaries like this to chart individual development. I have kept my observation notes for the first six months of Hannah's life. Here are some extracts:

> At 12 weeks Sam, her mother, said that Hannah had, by accident, hit the bell attached to an elephant mobile over her cot. She then repeated this action again and again, sometimes smiling at the bell and sometimes crying.
>
> At more or less the same time a friend came to see the new baby and brought with her her own five-year-old child, Jess – the first child Hannah had encountered. She sat on Jess's lap and really looked at the pictures in a book when Jess read it and at one point laughed out loud.
>
> When Sam wore a black and white striped shirt Hannah examined it moving her head from left to right. She was three months old at the time. At the same time she fell asleep with a smile on her face while she was having her bottle. When I noticed the smile and laughed she laughed out loud in her sleep. My observation notes record 'Delicious!'
>
> At nearly four months she turned to examine whoever was talking; smiled in anticipation when Sam started chanting 'The Owl and the Pussy Cat'; and when an adult counted '1, 2, 3 …' she waited with closed eyes in anticipation for whatever would follow. A diary entry for around this time says 'I

think she is genius (!!) because she looked from a Matisse cut-out in a book to a different Matisse cut-out on the wall.' At around the same time she communicated she wanted to play the game of having her feet lifted and dropped by stretching her legs and pointing her feet.

At four months Sam reported that when Hannah's dad counted '1, 2, 3 ... 4' Hannah (expecting a game) looked at him in utter disbelief. Sam said that Hannah has learned that changing the shape of her mouth affects the sounds she can make. 'I hear her practising vowel sounds in her cot at night.'

At five and a half months Hannah was doing lots of vocalising making the patterns of speech in her babbling. At the same time she showed great sensitivity to the moods of others, grinning at jolly Marion but shrieking at someone who was very tense with her.

At six months when she was first given water in a cup to drink she grasped it by the handles and immediately tilted it to get the water to her mouth.

As I read through these notes some 12 years later, a picture emerged of how this human infant was developing and of how she was beginning to make sense of her world. Equipped with some knowledge of theories of child development I am now able to analyse each little snippet to get an idea of just what it was that Hannah was doing alone and through the interactions she had with others in her world. Since this is a book about the great Russian theorist Lev Vygotsky, I aim to use these observations as a starting point for looking at some of his key ideas and complicated thoughts.

A Vygotskian analysis

At 12 weeks Sam, her mother, said that Hannah had, by accident, hit the bell attached to an elephant mobile over her cot. She then repeated this action again and again, sometimes smiling at the bell and sometimes crying.

It is tempting to think about this in fairly simple terms. By accident the child's foot rang the bell. The child liked the sound of the bell ringing and kept attempting to make the same thing happen again. But something is missing from that analysis. In order for the child to realise that she has caused the bell to ring the child has to have a sense of her own *agency* – her ability to make things happen in her immediate environment. And we are talking here of a child less than three months old. We will return to this notion of active learning and agency again and again. By active learning we mean that all human infants use all their senses and anything else available in order to understand their world and everything in it. They do it without having to be prompted to do so.

At more or less the same time a friend came to see the new baby and brought with her her own five-year-old child, Jess – the first child Hannah had encountered. She sat on Jess's lap and really looked at the pictures in a book when Jess read it and at one point laughed out loud.

Here we have a view of infant Hannah in *interaction* with a child – the first small being she had encountered. Jess already knew about books in the sense that she knew how books work and what people do in their interaction with books. So she knew to open the book and turn the pages and say the words and point to the pictures. Through this interaction with another person – an expert in terms of book behaviour – Hannah copied Jess in looking at the book and expressed her pleasure in the interaction with both Jess and the book through laughing aloud.

When Sam wore a black and white striped shirt Hannah examined it moving her head from left to right. She was three months old at the time.

It is intriguing to speculate what was happening here. What did black and white vertical lines suggest to her? Was there an interesting visual effect when she moved her head? Perhaps the lines seemed to move. Why did she move her head from left to right? It is tempting to suggest that Hannah was 'reading' the shirt, but perhaps that is stretching credulity. What we can say is that Hannah, as in all the observations, was *actively involved in making sense* of all aspects of her world and of the objects and people in it.

At the same time she fell asleep with a smile on her face while she was having her bottle. When I noticed the smile and laughed she laughed out loud in her sleep. My observation notes record 'Delicious!'

At nearly four months she turned to examine whoever was talking …

Here we see Hannah exploring and making sense of an aspect of the *social world* she inhabits. In the company of other people she has learned to pay attention to what they do and say and she has learned that different people have different voices. This allows her to monitor who is speaking and who not. And in doing this she is learning about speaking and listening; about taking turns, about conversations and about how spoken language sounds and works.

She smiled in anticipation when Sam started chanting 'The Owl and the Pussy Cat'.

Hannah lived in a home with parents who read books and listened to music. They often sang to her and she saw them involved with books and newspapers. One of the rituals in her family was the singing of songs or chanting of rhymes and poems. 'The Owl and the Pussy Cat' has a hypnotic rhythm and Hannah, from early on, would listen, entranced, to the whole poem. This was one of the *cultural tools* in her environment and something she used both for pleasure and for learning about aspects of *language* and of *interaction*. More than that this was part of her induction into the group of readers and the start of enabling her to participate in a particular *community of practice*.

> When an adult counted '1, 2, 3 ...' she waited with closed eyes in anticipation for whatever would follow.

Here we find the first sign of Hannah's ability to *predict* what might happen next. Through her experience of adults around her counting to three and then doing something dramatic (clapping hands, removing the towel from in front of the face, dropping a toy, turning on the light and so on) she has worked out that the sounds 'wuntoothree' work as the prelude to something exciting. She has discovered something we might call a pattern and uses this as a blueprint. Being able to predict is an essential skill. Some people might say that the *adults in her world are taking charge of her and moving her from being on the periphery of an activity to being at the centre of the activity.*

> A diary entry for around this time says 'I think she is genius (!!) because she looked from a Matisse cut-out in a book to a different Matisse cut-out on the wall'.

Remember that in the last entry we saw Hannah predicting. Here we see a really sophisticated example of a child starting to *generalise*. She was sitting on the lap of someone looking at a book in which there were examples of Matisse cut-outs, which are very brightly coloured and dramatic. She must have realised that something about them reminded her of a large picture hanging on the wall of the sitting room in her house. This was also a Matisse cut-out. Now this does not sound so complicated, but think about it. In order for a child to make this connection she had to be able to both *recall* something she had seen and *compare* that with something new she is looking at. Vygotsky would have talked of *higher mental functions*.

> At around the same time she communicated she wanted to play the game of having her feet lifted and dropped by stretching her legs and pointing her feet.

Now we see the first example of Hannah *communicating* her needs or wants to another person. Through her *experience* she has found that the game of having her feet lifted and dropped is pleasurable. She has also found that if she wants this to happen she needs to find a way of 'saying' so to someone. In the absence of speech she has to turn to the means available to her – the actions she can make. So she invents her own 'sentence' through this physical language – she stretches her legs and points her feet. Because the significant adults in her world – her mother or grandmother or father – are so tuned in to her needs and desires they become able to interpret her actions and respond to them. For Vygotsky thinking was a *culturally mediated social process of communication* and the social activity of speaking was connected to the active process of thinking. This is complicated stuff and we will return to it later in this book.

> At four months Sam reported that when Hannah's dad counted '1, 2, 3 … 4' Hannah (expecting a game) looked at him in utter disbelief.

Now Hannah shows that she is discovering that, although there are patterns and what you predict may happen, the world is more complex, the rules less rigid and people not always as they seem. Although her dad starts out the familiar pattern of '1, 2, 3…' he doesn't allow it to culminate in the expected surprise, but instead makes another sound. Perhaps he is moving her to another level of understanding here.

> Sam said that Hannah has learned that changing the shape of her mouth affects the sounds she can make. 'I hear her practising vowel sounds in her cot at night'.

The world Hannah lives in is full of the sounds of language. She is growing up in a monolingual home and so the sounds she hears are those of English. In a family down the road the children are hearing the sounds of English and of Bengali. Hannah shows that she has learned that her mouth, lips and tongue are involved in making her sounds and that adults around her also move their mouth, lips and tongue in order to talk. In her bed at night she makes a range of sounds which seem to be the sounds of English vowels. She is engaged in *imitation* and this has come about through her *interactions* with others.

> At five and a half months Hannah was doing lots of vocalising making the patterns of speech in her babbling.

Almost halfway through her first year Hannah is on the verge of joining her community of speakers and listeners. She practises not only the vowel sounds but also the patterned sounds of questions and statements. She is talking to herself, babbling away as she *imitates* others and *participates* in daily life.

> At the same time she showed great sensitivity to the moods of others, grinning at jolly Marion but shrieking at someone who was very tense with her.

In her short life Hannah has encountered many other people – adults, other infants and children. She has seen them smiling and frowning, laughing and crying, shouting and dancing, happy and sad, relaxed and tense. Through her observation of them and what is going on around them she has developed a sense of working out what it is that they feel. Doing this presupposes some awareness that other people have feelings. People like Judy Dunn (1988) who have looked at how children come to learn about the moods and feelings of others, agree that this happens in very early childhood and comes about through interactions as children work out their roles in the *rule-bound* social worlds they inhabit. Where she grinned with joy at Marion's antics, she was also silent in front of Sally who was withdrawn and tense. She was developing sensitivity to the moods of others.

> At six months when she was first given water in a cup to drink she grasped it by the handles and immediately tilted it to get the water to her mouth.

In this last entry from the diary we see Hannah *generalising* from her experience of drinking from a bottle to drinking from a cup. Again, what seems simple on the surface actually involves extremely complex thinking on behalf of this child. She realises that the cup is something you can drink from – just like a bottle – and like a bottle, the liquid can only reach your lips if the container is tilted.

You, the reader, are like Hannah in the sense that you are at the start of learning something new. This chapter gives you a very quick overview of some of the ideas of Lev Vygotsky, all of which we will explore in more detail throughout this book. The book is written in language designed to be accessible and it seeks to make some difficult concepts intelligible. You might want to remember that Vygotsky wrote originally in Russian so that all his work has been translated into English and there have been – and continue to be – disagreements among different translators as to how to convey most clearly his challenging ideas.

Chapter 1

Beginnings
Towards a sociohistorical appreciation

In this opening chapter we look at who Vygotsky was in terms of where and when he was born and what influences he encountered in his short life. Those who have written about his work describe it as *sociohistorical psychology* and by this they mean that he was convinced that to study human beings means to study them both in terms of their social relationships and experiences and according to the cultural tools used. Social experiences include things like the way in which others direct people's attention or model behaviour or praise or control or imitate or organise aspects of society like where and how people live (communally, in family units, and so on), how they eat, where they sleep. Cultural tools are the things or the signs or symbols that human beings within groups have developed over time in order to help them think about and reflect on their values, ideas, principles and practices. Cultural tools include, most importantly, language but also things like computers and music and art.

The life and times of Lev Vygotsky

Context and *culture* are two of the themes that underpin all his work. So to start our journey into his work let us learn something about his own life. He was born into an educated Jewish family in the small town of Orsha in what is now Belarus in 1896. A year later the family moved to the small and bustling city of Gomel, where his father, Semion, worked in a range of managerial positions and was at one time head of department in a bank. Semion was an important man in this small city, speaking several languages, and partly responsible for creating a library in the town. Much of what is known of Vygotsky's life comes from a paper written by his daughter, Gita Vygodskaya, who described her grandfather Semion as a difficult and complex man – determined, demanding and concerned for his children, attentive to their needs, and loving. His wife, Cecilia, was also well educated; she spoke German and had a love of German poetry, which she passed on to her children. By training she was a teacher, but since she gave birth to eight children it is no surprise to learn that she never actually taught formally, although she was, of course, deeply involved in the education of her children. Lev was the second child in the family, but the first son. All the children worked hard to care for one another and to keep the family together. Gita says they were united by a shared interest in and love of history, literature, theatre and art. She says,

> It was a family tradition to get together after the evening tea. By this time everyone was done with his or her activities, the father with business, the mother with housework and the children with their school assignments. They then talked amongst themselves about whatever came to mind, or read aloud either classic novels or newly released ones. Both the parents and children valued this time of family closeness and spoke warmly of it for many years to come.
>
> (Vygodskaya 1995)

We get the sense of a loving and vibrant family life where discussion of ideas and events was part of the cultural habitus. Gita tells us that although money was tight there was always money for books. Lev was said to be sociable and popular, with a passion for stamp collecting, chess, reading adventure stories, swimming and boating. His first brush with education was in the home, being taught by tutors and studying on his own. He then went on to secondary school, the Jewish gymnasium, where he was taught by Solomon Ashpiz, a mathematician who had spent some time in exile in Siberia for taking part in what were called 'revolutionary activities'.

Young Lev started his life in pre-revolutionary Russia, where the country was ruled by the tsars and the poor were exceedingly poor and ill educated. Anti-semitism was rife and it is evident that the Vygotsky family were not exempt from the consequences of this. Kozulin (1990) tells us that after a trivial incident at a farmers' market in Gomel there was a full-scale pogrom against the homes and businesses of some of Gomel's Jews. It seems that, unlike Jews elsewhere who did not defend themselves, the Jewish community of Gomel resisted and in a few cases managed to defeat their attackers. A number of Jews were brought to trial after this terrible incident, and the trial became a platform for a public confrontation between those who wanted full rights for minority groups and pro-government groups who were keen to place all blame on the Jews. Vygotsky's father was called as a witness to testify about the atmosphere in the town on the eve of the pogrom. In his testimony he talked about an earlier pogrom in Kishenev and suggested that terrible incidents like these were likely to continue as long as Jews insisted on their human dignity and civil rights. Lev was only eight years old at this time and it is certain that what he saw and heard influenced him throughout the rest of his short life.

It seems that he flourished at the gymnasium: his teachers were impressed with his abilities and predicted a brilliant future for him – some as a mathematician, others as a philologist. Favourable comments were made about his seriousness and his maturity. He did so well in the end-of-school exams that he graduated in 1913 with a gold medal. He applied to Moscow University knowing that the government imposed a quota system for Jews but confident despite this that his good grades would gain him entry. His parents hoped he would become a doctor because in doing so he would be able to live beyond the Pale – that is, outside the few provinces where Jews were allowed to live permanently. Having dutifully – and successfully – applied to study medicine, Vygotsky realised within less than a month of commencing his studies that he really did not want to study medicine and transferred to Moscow University's Law School. Once again his studies did not please him. He was determined to follow up his interests in languages, literature, art and philosophy. He took the decision to transfer to Shanavsky's University, also in Moscow, a progressive institution that paid no heed to the nationality or ethnicity of students but was not recognised as a legitimate organisation. Although the teaching was said to be excellent the degrees granted by this university were not officially recognised.

His time as a student in Moscow was a happy and busy one. And it was during these formative years that his keen interest in psychology developed and he began to study it in his own time and largely through his own efforts. Part of his work at university required that he submit a thesis. He chose to write his thesis on Shakespeare's play, *Hamlet*. He spent years analysing the play and examining its many translations. The resulting thesis was his first piece of scientific research. If you are familiar with the play you will know that it is primarily about the complexities of relationships between people, about power, about the past and about madness. Clearly his growing interest in psychology was instrumental in his choice of topic or, perhaps, his interest in *Hamlet* determined his passion for psychology. You may be interested to know that his thesis was eventually published fifty years later, appearing as an addendum to a 1968 edition of his *Psychology of Art*.

Vygotsky finished his education at university in the fateful year of 1917 and returned to Gomel. The impact of the Great War on Russia had been terrible: millions had died of starvation, and troops had been sent into battle too poorly equipped to combat either the enemy or the weather. He found Gomel occupied by German forces, and it was impossible for him to find a job at this time. He also found his family facing terrible traumas. His mother was recovering from a bout of tuberculosis, as was one of his younger brothers. The boy was in a critical state, and Lev was involved in nursing him until the boy died before his fourteenth birthday. His mother was still struggling to recover both from her own illness and her bereavement when a second brother died, this time of typhoid fever. The October Revolution in 1918 was a hugely significant moment in the history of the country – indeed, of the world. For Lev, the beginning of a socialist government allowed him to work and to study. He, like other members of minority groups, began to feel entitled to dignity and respect and although, over the years, he had his disagreements with aspects of Marxism, the impact of Marxism is evident in some of his views. In 1919 he began to teach literature, philosophy and Russian in a newly opened vocational school. He later taught psychology in a local teacher training college. He became head of art and aesthetic education in the town council and spent much of his life developing culture and education. These, together with literature and theatre, remained his life's passions. Some time later he was nominated as the best teacher in Gomel.

Later he turned his attention to research and in doing this came across Alexander Luria, with whom he found he had much in common. He also met Alexei Leontiev and the three men worked happily together in what they called a 'troika' or threesome. Soon after this he began to work in a centre for physically disabled children and those who were described as 'mentally retarded'. In 1925 he had the honour of attending a conference in London to present his country's work on the education of 'deaf and mute' children. He took full advantage of the chance to travel through Europe and spent time examining provision for special education in Holland, France and Germany. On his return to Russia he fell ill with tuberculosis and nearly died. But as he struggled to regain his health he continued researching and writing and some of his work was published. Some of this related to the education of children with special needs and what was remarkable about this was that he consulted the children themselves. It was this, perhaps, that made him turn his attention to pedagogy – the art or the science of teaching. What he was doing aroused so much interest that teachers, doctors, students and psychologists from all over Moscow rushed to the conferences and lectures he held – and those who could not fit into the lecture theatre listened from outside, held by his ideas and views. What made him so remarkable was the attention he paid to the views of the child and the respect he accorded all children. We also know that he married and had children and that his wife survived him by 45 years. His daughter, Gita, and granddaughter, Eleni, are both still alive.

The intellectual impact of others on Vygotsky's thinking

We are all the sum total of our experiences and our interactions with the people and the ideas and the cultural tools we encounter throughout our lives. We are all influenced by other people and their ideas and values throughout our lives. Often the influence comes about through seeing some people as role models or through wanting to do something that someone we admire does. For many people the influence comes not directly through interactions with people but from learning of their thoughts and ideas through reading or listening. Perhaps in your life you have been influenced by the ideas of some of your teachers or your friends or members of your family. Perhaps a book you have read or a talk you have attended has made you think differently. Perhaps you have heard of the work of remarkable individuals and that has had some impact on your life.

Consider George Bizos, a South African lawyer. As a small boy, he and his father had to flee the country of his birth, Greece, while it was under Nazi occupation, rowing across the Mediterranean until picked up by a British destroyer. He was only 12 at the time but the memory stayed with him throughout his life, first in an orphanage and later in South Africa, where he completed his schooling and became an advocate. His early experiences enabled him to identify with the wrongs he encountered in apartheid South Africa, and he later became known as a passionate defender of the rights of the oppressed, including, among others, Nelson Mandela.

Or consider the experiences of Primo Levi when, as a young Italian in Auschwitz, he drew on what he had learned in his undergraduate chemistry degree to help him cope with the impossible demands and inhuman encounters in that camp. In *The Drowned and the Saved* Levi wrote:

> Together with the baggage of practical notions I had got from my studies, I had brought along with me into the Lager an ill-defined patrimony of mental habits which derive from chemistry and its environs, but have broader applications. If I act in a certain way, how will the substance I hold in my hands react, or my human interlocutor? Why does it or he or she manifest or interrupt or change a specific behaviour? Can I anticipate what will happen around me in one minute or tomorrow or in a month? If so, which are the signs that matter, which those to neglect? Can I foresee the blow, know from which side it will come, parry it, elude it?
>
> (1988: 113–14)

Later in the same passage, which looked at what happened to intellectuals in the Lager, Levi argued that the camp itself operated as a 'university' in the sense that it taught him (and others) to look around and to measure men. So Levi reflected on how his formal education and his desperate experiences both contributed to the sum total of who he became.

Vygotsky himself was, in some senses, an 'outsider'. Growing up as a Jew, surrounded by anti-semitism, pogroms and racial laws, he devoted his life to ideas which, in essence, examined society and history, and whilst doing that led him to start to explore more closely how those around him learned and developed their own sets of values and beliefs and practices. The culture in which he lived was one which reflected the negative values and practices outlined above. What was particular about his approach was his focus on the social and the cultural.

Vygotsky lived through dramatic and stimulating times and became part of what is known as the Russian *intelligentsia*. This is a concept that does not translate easily into English because we do not have a comparable group of people. Kozulin (1999: 21) tells us that the intelligentsia did not comprise just educated classes or just intellectual people. Rather it was a group of people united not only by a common set of cultural values and a deep sense of social justice but also by the desire to work towards the betterment of society as a whole. In the intelligentsia at that time literature was held in extremely high regard and thought to be the ultimate expression of culture and of life itself. So literary characters were discussed and judged in terms of how those who read about these characters could use them and their actions as models for their own lives. You can see something of this in the thesis Vygotsky wrote on *Hamlet* referred to earlier.

Vygotsky completed his studies in 1917 when he graduated and returned to Gomel. As you may know this was the year of the Russian Revolution which transformed the nature of society within the then Russian empire, transforming the old tsarist autocracy into what became the Soviet Union. During that year there were two revolutions. The February Revolution was a spontaneous popular uprising in the city of Petrograd. This could not be sustained initially, largely because of the impact of the First World War on the economy and on the country. The October Revolution which followed was where the workers, led by Lenin, managed to take control. They introduced a programme designed to rid the country of the aristocracy, educate the populace, ensure that wealth was more equitably shared and give land to the poor. Those in power fiercely resisted and in the chaos that followed a bitter civil war took place.

Vygotsky thus returned to Gomel at a time of rifts and divisions all around him as the nation accommodated to a new way of organising society. The move from the feudal society of the tsars to a socialist order was one of the most rapid and dramatic changes in history. At the time there were thought to be two distinct groupings – those who wanted no change and were known as archaists and those who wanted as much change as quickly as possible, the innovators. Many of the innovators were interested in the concept of *objectification*. This is a difficult concept to explain and understand but important for us in terms of Vygotsky's later work on mediation.

To try and explain it let us start with a concrete example. If someone shows you a table or a picture of a table you immediately know what it is and can name it. You don't have to think about it. You just know. But perhaps you know what it is through your experience of seeing a table used for one purpose or another or using a table yourself for one purpose or another. You know what a table is according to the meaning the table has for you. For you it is perhaps the place where you eat your meals, or at which you sit with your laptop, or where you place a bowl of flowers. One way of coming to understand objectification is to consider whether something is merely an object or whether it is imbued with meaning as a result of why it was made and whatever its purpose is. A table, you might think, is just something made of wood. But then so is a wooden bowl or a wooden tray. We understand that the table is the table precisely because it was produced by humans for particular purposes. So a table or any other object becomes something imbued with meaning according to the purposes for which it was designed and made. The bowl was made to hold fruit or salad. The tray was made to carry things on. So objectification is the process by which people assign meaning to things, or to people, or to places, or to activities, or, in the case of self-objectification, to themselves. These meanings thus become part of cultural constructions which inform and guide behaviour. We continue to use the table to eat on or to work at or to place objects on. We – the people in our groups or communities or cultures – assign meaning and we do this through a process known as cultural construction. Cultural constructions are arbitrary in that they are created and maintained by each culture. So they are not fixed for ever; rather, they are dynamic and change over time and through space. Here is a small example to illustrate this.

In one of the first books to come out of the wonderful nurseries in Reggio Emilia in Italy was a photograph of a small child turning the pages of a catalogue and putting her ear against the picture of a wrist watch. She was expecting it to tick. In a sense she was demonstrating her ability to generalise from the watches she had seen and using her expectation that all watches make a noise. She had not yet learned that a picture of a watch cannot make a noise. Nowadays that photograph would be meaningless because watches no longer tick. They are digital. So our cultural construction of timepieces has had to adapt. A watch still measures time but operates in a different way.

At the same time that Vygotsky's thinking was being shaped by his experiences in the new socialist world there were many individuals whose thoughts and ideas and research and interactions influenced his thinking throughout his life. One of the earliest and most significant influences in his life (as it was on Karl Marx also) was the work of the philosopher Hegel. As a Jewish student in Russia Vygotsky was trying to understand and explain anti-semitism as a concept and in doing that he wanted to understand what it was within Jewish culture that seemed to be a threat to others and what laws governed history as a process to allow this discrimination to surface over and over again over time. This meant that he had to explore the concepts of both culture and history. In his work Hegel had written about both concepts in an approach that can be described as *dialectical*. The word *dialectic* comes from the Greek and refers to a controversy where there is both an argument and a counter-argument. So it means the coming together of two opposing views. Put more simply it means not accepting that one thing is true and the opposite false, but trying to see how each contributes to an understanding. In his attempt to analyse history Hegel had been concerned to describe the development of man and in doing that he talked of reason, of culture, of consciousness, and of will. (Here we can say that reason means logical thinking; culture means developing shared customs, values, beliefs and so on; consciousness means awareness; and will means desire or motivation.) The underpinning law of history for Hegel was that it was made up of man's progression towards a consciousness (or an awareness) of freedom. So history was seen not as linear but as involving leaps forward, obstacles encountered, returns and detours made and negotiations offered. In order to move ahead some obstacles have to be encountered and overcome. So history is dialectical.

Another important aspect of Hegel's work that was to have considerable influence on Vygotsky was his distinction between the *natural world* and *the world of culture*. This is still a fiercely debated area of philosophy where different thinkers believe that all culture (meaning things made by man) is rooted in nature. For our purposes the natural world refers to the things that are here as physical entities and have come about through evolution and development: trees, human beings, rocks and stones, mountains and seas, flowers and volcanoes. The cultural world refers to the world where groups of people have developed their own artefacts or objects and ideas and practices to meet their group needs. Vygotsky saw the world of culture in just this way, defining it as the work of groups in society who construct values and ideologies, religions and artefacts, customs and practices that then come to define them and link them to one another. If you remind yourself of objectification – how objects are defined by the purposes for which they were made or the purposes assigned them by people – you will not be surprised to learn that he was also interested in objectification. When he started to think about how children learn you will find him talking about how they begin to assign meaning to objects. As you read on you will see how much emphasis Vygotsky put on the importance of the social and cultural worlds in the learning and development of humans.

For Vygotsky all learning was social. This is a contentious idea, and the first time you read this statement you might feel outraged, remembering the many occasions when you learned something on your own, without any help, perhaps by waking up in the middle of the night with a 'Eureka!' moment. But think about this. He meant social in the sense that ideas and concepts are often mediated by more experienced learners; that learning takes place in a context which may well be social in origin; that learning builds on previous learning; and that learning takes place primarily through cultural and psychological tools. We will return to this again and again in this book. If you are particularly interested in the influence of Hegel on Vygotsky you should read Kozulin's book (1999).

Other influences on Vygotsky included Alexander Luria and Alexei Leontiev. You will recall that they formed a group and called themselves the 'troika' or threesome. They were both young members of the Institute of Psychology at Moscow State University when Vygotsky met them. Luria was an experienced researcher who was seeking to come up with what he called an 'objective' approach to understanding unconscious emotional processes and Leontiev was a doctoral student. The three met once or twice a week to plan their own research programme. Vygotsky at that time was immersed in considering the devastating effects of recent history (this was in the 1920s and the country had been through a civil war, the Great War, occupation and famine, and then the first years of communist rule). He became involved in studying the effects of newly introduced compulsory secondary education and this led him to consider how to offer emotional and psychological support to those who found this difficult to cope with. The troika was later joined by five other researchers, some of whom were women, and the work of this group was truly collective. Vygotsky was the nominal leader but each of the members was free to use one another's ideas to influence their own findings.

One of the research projects was Luria's study of urban, rural and homeless children. His research question was whether different social experiences would bring about not only different knowledge but would stimulate different types of mental (or thought) processes. He selected three groups of children aged between nine and 12 years and from three groups: one from a large city (probably Moscow); one from a remote rural village and the third a group of homeless urchins. All of the 130 participants were given simple word association tasks. He analysed the responses trying to find a pattern within and between the groups.

Think about the words 'cart' and 'union'. The word 'cart' is one which we might expect to be more familiar to rural than to urban children and indeed it was evident that rural children responded more uniformly than urban children, giving responses like 'something to ride in'. 'Union', on the other hand, produced strikingly different responses in that rural children drew on their own associations relating to cooperative unions which have shops. Town children, on the other hand, gave responses indicating an awareness of a union as a social concept and produced associations like 'worker', or 'councils' or 'youth'.

The research probably suggests that those with more varied experience, and experience involving the thoughts and ideas of others, are more likely to be able to do things like generalise and analyse. Following this rather simplistic research Vygotsky and Luria went on to carry out a much more complex piece of research relating to how changes in cultural environment lead to changes in cognition. Their research group consisted of Uzbeks who had been drawn from an almost feudal system into the new socialist republic. In a very rapid transition which involved being introduced to enormous changes such as mass education and propaganda, rights for women and so on, they could be conceived of as a group likely to reveal the changes both Vygotsky and Luria expected. The research was revealing and interesting but was heavily criticised for many years by those who said it did nothing but ascribe 'primitive thinking' to non-literate or poorly educated people.

During one phase of the research Luria reported finding that the perceptions of colour were different in Uzbek peasants and Uzbek teachers and administrators. When presented with cow dung and pig dung the peasants were clear that they were different because they came from different animals. The teachers and administrators were able to abstract the concept 'colour' and describe both as being brown. When the results were published the political system reprimanded the researchers, saying the differences they found were racist and went against the ideals of socialism and equity. They were forbidden from publishing their results and Luria was expelled from the Institute of Psychology at Moscow State University.

Looking back, looking ahead

By the time of Vygotsky's death in 1934 Stalin was in charge and the society Vygotsky inhabited had changed enormously. His death, after a final dose of tuberculosis at the tender age of 37, left a void which was never filled. His work was not translated into English until the 1960s and early translators argued fiercely about their individual interpretations of his views. But the impact of his work spread throughout the world. He left behind books and articles and a legacy so rich that it is still being argued over and explained today.

You now know something about Vygotsky's brief life and about the family, the community and the society in which he spent this life. This gives you a context for considering his ideas. What you have read may have suggested some questions to you. Perhaps you wonder how much peer teaching he did of his own siblings. After all, in a family of eight children it is very likely that teaching one another was common practice. Was this, in any way, important in the development of his thinking about teaching and learning? You may wonder what impact the discrimination he and his family and community suffered had on his ideas and thinking. Or maybe you will question how his work with children we might define as having special needs determined the direction of his own thinking and the conclusions he drew. The importance of this will become clearer as you read on.

You also have a window on some of his ideas and of the terminology we will use to talk about children's learning and development. If you re-read the analysis of Hannah's behaviour you will find words and phrases such as *interaction*, *social world*, *cultural tools*, *communication*, *language*, *community of practice*, *imitation*, *participation*, *higher mental functions* and *mediation*. Each of these terms includes some reference to the roles of others. The prominence of the social, embedded in these terms, is an indication that the way in which Vygotsky saw children and learning was one that focused on how learning is passed on from one generation to another through relationships and interactions – a view that is both social and historical.

A glossary of terms

Before you read on please note the glossary of terms that follows this and every chapter in this book. Just like any learner new to something, coming to terms with the specialised language of your new area of study takes time. Vygotsky's work is difficult to read and, critically, to understand – probably for Russian speakers as well as English speakers – because he uses terms that often are not the currency of everyday speech. Some of the words which appear in italics in the text are explained in the glossary. Some of them are also explained in terms of their significance for those of us working with young children. They are arranged in alphabetical order. Do look them up.

Glossary

Word or phrase	What it means	Why it is significant
active learning	A learner not being passively filled with information or knowledge but actively trying to make sense of all experiences and encounters.	We cannot treat learners as blank slates or empty vessels but must engage with them as partners in a dialogue.

agency	This refers to the ability and need for learners to be in control of their own learning.	We have to take account of what it is that interests the learner and offer opportunities within schools and settings for learners to build on their interests and passions.
communicate	The ability of people to interact and exchange ideas.	Extremely important in that almost all learning involves communication.
community of practice	This refers to people who are all involved in the same activity. We could think about how a child is inducted into the community of practice of the playground or into the community of readers.	This has implications for us in terms of how we introduce new things to the children and ensure we take them from being on the edge to being part of the group.
compare	An everyday word meaning looking for what is the same and what is not the same in objects or situations.	One of the higher mental functions that children acquire through experience and interactions.
consciousness	This means awareness of something.	
context	Often used to refer to where things take place. The context of learning could be in the setting or the classroom or the home or the playground, for example.	Context is very important because it is where meaning is made and shared.
cultural habitus	A term used by Bourdieu to describe what we all learn from others in our groups.	Important for us to consider in our planning for children in order that we offer appropriate resources, activities and interactions.

cultural tools	Sometimes referred to as psychological tools these are the objects and signs and systems developed by human beings over time and within communities to assist thinking. They include things like language, symbols, music, art and others.	All learners come from cultures which have developed their own cultural tools. Children need access to tools that allow them to use them to make sense of the world.
culture	Difficult to define but in general it refers to the ways in which groups of people pass on beliefs and values and the products of human work and thought.	Because Vygotsky was interested in how knowledge was both constructed and passed on from one generation to another he was deeply concerned with how this was dependent on culture.
developmental diary	A set of observation notes, sometimes supported by photographs or recordings, charting the development of a child. Often kept by parents.	Observing children and taking notes of what is seen and heard is an essential tool for any educator.
dialectical	This is a term used to think about the position where someone does not come down on one side or another but seeks to argue both sides.	Vygotsky was interested in analysing phenomena from more than one perspective.
experience	Another everyday term meaning everything that has been seen, heard, felt, understood, appreciated.	All experience is valuable and children learn from all their experiences. We, as educators, need to have this as our starting point.
generalise	A familiar term meaning the ability to draw from an individual case to the general.	A higher order function developed by children through experience and interactions.
imitation	An everyday word which describes what happens when one person copies the behaviour or actions of another.	Imitation plays a role in learning although cannot account for how learners are able to construct their own understanding.

intelligentsia	A Russian word used to describe people who share views and values, often related to their culture and language but also to human rights.	
interact	Where people are together in pairs or larger groups and exchanging thoughts, ideas, words, and experiences.	In a social model of learning like that of Vygotsky interaction is seen as an essential feature of learning.
language	A word that needs no explanation and refers to the most powerful of all cultural tools, encompassing speaking and listening, reading and writing. Sometimes also used for non-verbal ways of communicating.	The most important way in which ideas and thoughts are shared and meanings negotiated. A key feature of the nature of all education and learning.
natural world	This means the world of things that came about through growth and evolution and not the world of things made by humans.	
making sense	Children, from before birth, use every means available to them to understand the physical and social and emotional world in which they live.	We are concerned, all the time, with helping children make sense of all aspects of their lives and experience.
mediated	This means something that acts as a facilitator to learning, that moves between the learner and the concept to be learned. The definition may change as you keep reading.	Mediation is key to Vygotsky's thoughts and this is firmly rooted in his view as being essentially social and cultural.
objectification	The process by which an object acquires meaning.	A reminder that learners need access to the concrete and the everyday in order to be able to think abstractly.

participate	An everyday word meaning to join in.	Participation is essential for children and adults. Children need to join in with the culture and activities of their settings and adults need to participate with children.
predict	An everyday word meaning the ability to guess what will happen next.	A higher mental function.
recall	An everyday word meaning the ability to remember.	A higher mental function.
rule-bound	This applies to things like language which is held together with rules in order for everyone speaking the language to be able to both use and understand it. There are many rule-bound systems which are part of our cultural tools.	As you read on you will find that children from very early on invent their own rules and apply them to monitor their own behaviour.
sensitivity to the moods of others	This refers to the ability of people to feel and respond to the moods of those people whom they encounter.	We should be attentive to children doing this.
social world	Those who are involved with the child in all the child's various contexts and cultures.	
sociohistorical	The approach of Vygotsky, which was one which thought it essential to consider the history and the culture from which anything arose.	It is vital for us to know as much as possible about the child's individual history and culture.

Chapter 2

On mediation, memory and cultural tools

In this chapter we start to think about how children learn and develop within the framework suggested by Vygotsky, that is, within what he called 'cultural', 'historical' or 'instrumental' psychology. The focus of this chapter is on mediation and this involves us beginning to consider the complex and fascinating area of memory and the use of cultural tools. To lead us into the discussion we will first define a number of terms.[1]

The cultural, historical and instrumental framework

By *cultural* Vygotsky meant the socially structured ways in which society organises the many tasks the growing child encounters and the tools, which may be mental (which means internal or psychological) or physical (which means external or material), that the young child is provided with to master those tasks. For example, in Western societies we often organise a room for the new baby, equipped with special furniture and other things thought to be necessary for the baby to thrive. The child may have a mobile hanging over the cot and toys to handle. In Africa, a separate bedroom with a cot and a change mat and toys would often be unheard of. The new baby might sleep in a lined box or with the parents. These are cultural differences and do not indicate that one is better than the other in terms of helping children learn and develop. The Western child might explore a soft toy while the African child explores a pine cone. Both children are coming to understand their worlds through their own explorations. But what is shared is that this learning usually takes place within a social context, alongside others, and is often bathed in language which, for Vygotsky, is the primary cultural tool.

By *historical* Vygotsky meant how humans have mastered and used the environment – and continue to do so – over decades. Using language as an example we can think of how language carries within it the generalised concepts that make up the sum of human knowledge. The new baby in a Western home will probably have books read to him and rhymes chanted. A baby in Africa might have stories told rather than read. The very word 'stories' carries within it an indication of what

---

1. In order to simplify the reading and understanding of this chapter we will refer to cultural tools and not to psychological tools when we talk of the systems and processes and things created by people within groups over time.

stories are and refers implicitly to all the stories known to those within a particular culture. The concept 'historical' is closely linked to the concept 'cultural' and we need to consider as part of history cultural tools such as writing and mathematics and music, which have been developed by us as humans and which expand our power to analyse the present, make sense of the past and predict the future.

By *instrumental* Vygotsky was talking about *mediation* – which is central to Vygotsky's theory. Mediation refers to the use of cultural tools or signs to bring about qualitative changes in thinking. So we can talk of mediation as the use of *communicable systems* for representing reality as well as for acting on it. Communicable systems are ways of sharing thoughts and ideas: language is a communicable system. An important thing to consider is that mediation goes beyond thinking about learning in terms of stimulus–response. You may have read about the work of the Nobel Prize-winning Russian physiologist, Ivan Pavlov, whose research into digestion often involved studying the behaviour of dogs. He realised that salivation was an essential part of digestion and decided to see whether dogs could be made to respond to an artificial external stimulus – a metronome. So he started off by ringing the metronome at the same time as giving the dogs food. After several days the dogs began to salivate when they heard the ringing of the metronome, even before any food was present. Pavlov called this a conditional reflex, and his ideas were very influential in the formulation of stimulus–response theory: the stimulus in this case was the sound of the metronome, and the response – salivation in the absence of food – was a changed behaviour. Some over-enthusiastic psychologists decided to apply this approach to human development. It was suggested that reward and punishment could be used to change behaviour: reward a child with a smiley face and the child will continue to do whatever was praised; take away the child's toy and the child will stop the unacceptable behaviour. This will be familiar to you and is based on a very simplistic view of learning, one that was totally against that of Vygotsky.

Memory, mediation and cultural tools

Don't panic if you haven't yet understood what is meant by mediation. It is a difficult concept to grasp and we will return to it again and again throughout this book. Mediation is the use of ways of communicating, primarily through signs and symbols, in order to understand and explain or represent the world and our experiences in it. In order to understand this more fully let's ensure that you are familiar with the meanings of the terms *sign* and *symbol*:

- A *sign* is a combination of meaning and form. The form of a road sign, for example, is something made of metal and the meaning relates to some information or warning about roads and/or traffic. A triangular road sign stands for danger.
- A *symbol* encapsulates and conveys meaning. The numeral 2 means more than one and less than three; the letters c-a-t mean an animal (cat) and the red cross indicates a place where help for the injured or sick can be found.

Human beings have developed many different ways of communicating their thoughts and ideas about the world, and they have used signs and symbols in their communicative systems. As they develop ways of communicating the ways of communicating themselves also change thinking and understanding. For example, think about how seeing a film (which is not reality but a series of moving images sometimes bound by language and used to represent aspects of reality) can sometimes change what you think about something. The film is an artefact built up of signs and symbols. You may also be changed through reading a book or talking to a friend or going to a lecture. So the ways of communicating change the ways in which we think. The ways of communicating can also be called *cultural tools*. One of the most important things about cultural tools is that they allow us to think about things when the things themselves are no longer present. We can remember a film we watched in the cinema last night, or a book we read last summer or a talk we had with a friend weeks ago. You begin to get a sense here of the link between thought, cultural tools and *memory*.

Let us start by looking at some of the more obvious tools people use to help them remember things when the things are not actually present. Think about the small examples below and in each case consider what it is you feel the named person is doing which could be called 'mediation'.

> Martha is about to go to the supermarket. She has a lot to buy and she makes herself a list to ensure that she remembers everything.

Martha is using the cultural tool of writing (developed by man over centuries and used to facilitate memory and learning) in order to remind her what to buy.

> Parveen is new to the nursery class. He spends part of each day of the first week wandering around the perimeter fence of the garden saying out loud, 'Here is the road. This is the corner. There is the climbing frame. Now I am on the grass. Here is the gate.'

Parveen is using the cultural tool of speech (developed and refined and elaborated by man over generations) in order to help him become familiar with a new and potentially threatening environment. He could equally well have drawn a picture of the nursery or just talked to his mum about it. Both also use cultural tools (making a pictorial image or using the spoken word) to mediate his learning of a new context.

> Xian is learning to play the recorder and has to learn to both name and play the notes written in the treble clef (in musical notation). In order to remember the names of the notes that sit on the lines of the treble clef Xian is given a mnemonic device by his older sister: EGBDF – 'Every Good Boy Deserves Food'.

Xian is using a *mnemonic* (a psychological tool for remembering, where the initial letter is used to stand for a word in a sentence, based on the idea that remembering something with a meaning is easier than remembering the names of letters). He has learned this from his older sister who, no doubt, learned it from another more experienced learner.

We have all developed symbols and ways of problem-solving which, in their turn, shape our thinking. From birth you will know that children are almost always in interaction with others, particularly with adults, who actively seek to draw the child into their culture and into the historically accumulated store of meanings and ways of doing things. Here are some examples to consider.

> Sacha's dad tells him stories from Russia, in Russian, while his mum sings him English songs and plays lots of predictive games which always end with a surprise.

This child is being inducted into the cultural store of the cultures of both his parents.

> Xoliswe carries her baby on her back and the baby observes all aspects of daily life. Often Xoliswe tells the baby what she is doing, even though the baby is only three months old.

Xoliswe's baby is being drawn into the rituals of her mother's culture through being physically present and being talked to throughout daily routines.

> At school the older children are sometimes invited to come into the garden of the nursery class to play ring games with the younger ones.

Older children, in this case, are inducting younger ones into the playground games and rituals of that school.

The move from physical needs and biological processes to higher mental functions.

As children grow and develop their lives become less dominated by physical needs and biological processes. Soon after birth babies' lives are dominated by their physical needs – sleep, food, warmth. As they begin to grow, and following their interactions with others, they begin to move away from these physiological needs to looking and listening and feeling and experiencing. They begin to actively find out about their worlds. Through their interactions with others their own thinking develops. In the language of Vygotsky, they are developing *higher order mental functions* such as the ability to compare, to order, to analyse, to remember and to generalise. (You came across some of these in the Glossary at the end of Chapter 1.) The process of development seems, then, to move from an initial stage in which the child's responses to the world are dominated by natural processes to a stage where more complex and instrumental processes begin to happen through the constant intervention of adults. The child has her attention drawn to the snow falling outside, or she hears words said over and over again, or she is given a plastic duck in the bath, or a book to look at, or a finger of bread to chew on. Vygotsky said that adults, at this stage, are acting as the external agents mediating the children's contact with the world and the people and objects in it. With time and experience the processes that were initially shared with adults come to be performed by the children themselves. The child points to the plastic duck as soon as the bathwater is run, or crawls to the window to look out, or keeps bringing a picture book to her mother. This is an extremely important point and you may need to read this several times for it to become clear to you.

Vygotsky would have said that initially the processes were *interpsychological*, which means they were shared between child and adult (*inter-* means 'between'). Later they become *intrapsychological*, which means that children can respond to the world on their own (*intra-* means 'within'). Cole (1996) tried to explain this using diagrams to illustrate the role of mediation in the process of a child learning to read. The diagrams below are based on his models.

These diagrams show how the child's experience of the world is mediated through her interactions with adults or more experienced others (Figure 2.1), but the adult or more expert learner has already learned more about the world through the mediation of cultural tools – in this case, text (Figure 2.2). The child eventually becomes able to use text or other cultural tools to mediate her experience of the world (Figure 2.3). There seems to me to be a gap here and that is the gap showing how the adult and child, together, use text to mediate experience before the child is able to internalise this. So my diagram to show this (Figure 2.4) illustrates the stage of pedagogy or teaching and should actually appear between Figures 2.2 and 2.3.

Figure 2.1 The experience of the world that children have mediated by adults or more expert others

26 Sandra Smidt

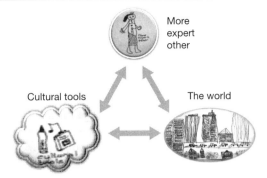

Figure 2.2 The experiences of the world that more expert others have mediated by text or other cultural tools

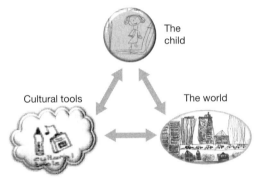

Figure 2.3 The goal of instruction – in this case the child's experience of the world mediated by text or other cultural tools

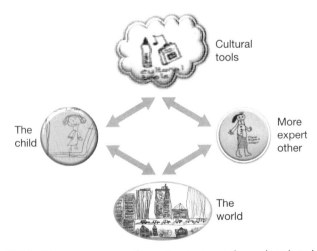

Figure 2.4 Child with more expert other using text or other cultural tools to mediate experience. This should come between Figures 2.1 and 2.3, since it is what enables the child alone to use cultural tools to mediate experience

From everyday thinking to higher mental functions

We have been discussing how, through mediation and the use of cultural tools, children move from dependence on others and on concrete and everyday experience to being able to remember, internalise and use this experience independently. This is the road from everyday mental functions to higher mental functions. Some interpreters of Vygotsky's work think that a central principle for him was this transition from lower or elementary mental functions to higher mental functions. Let us take a little time now to think about this in more detail.

Vygotsky drew a distinction between lower and higher mental processes in the following way:

- Lower mental processes are aspects of how we function such as memory, attention and intelligence; they are regarded as being *psychobiological* in origin and include things like reflexes. 'Psychobiological' means that these processes are thought to relate to feelings and emotions, and links between biological, social, cultural and environmental factors are important.
- Higher functions are *conscious* (and that is crucial) and include things like making deliberate intentional movements, consciously paying attention to something, and putting things into categories. They are related to things like verbal thinking, logical reasoning and selective attention.

In effect Vygotsky was talking about what we might call the differences between more concrete and more abstract thinking. And you now know that the way in which children reach higher mental functions is through *mediated, social, collaborative activity*.

You will not be surprised to learn that for Vygotsky higher mental processes are a function of socially meaningful activity. This is an extremely important point. What he is saying is that higher mental functions come about through *activity* where the young child is busy exploring something that has some meaning or relevance for him or her. We more commonly use the word 'experience' for activity. Here are some examples, all drawn from Karmiloff-Smith (1994) and all submitted by parents who were keeping developmental diaries of their own children.

> Genevieve (nineteen months): This week I gave her a bottle of juice during a meal. When she had finished I brought a second with milk. She put the two side by side and said 'two'. Other times she has simply repeated my last word but this time the 'two' was not a mimic of what I said.
>
> (Karmiloff-Smith 1994: 174)

Through her interactions with her mother during meal times (a social and meaningful activity) this little girl has had experience of being given one thing and then another. This appears to have been mediated by the mother talking to the child about what was happening – drawing the child into the routine of numbers and counting. So the child, having heard the word 'two', has internalised it and used it appropriately by herself. She has heard the word, remembered it and used it on her own in a meaningful way.

> Marko (thirteen months): This last week Marko has decided to push every button in the house to see what it does. If it does something, he does it again and again. He especially likes the CD player which has an 'ON' button because when he pushes it he gets a little light show.
> (Karmiloff-Smith 1994: 181)

Marko, through fairly random activity (pushing buttons) has discovered that some buttons, when pressed, do something that interests and pleases him. So he repeats the activity. In order to do this he has to have generalised the concept of 'pushing buttons' and selected from this the buttons which produce a result that pleased him. Making a choice is a higher mental process.

> Theo (ten months): He copied me brushing my hair the other day, and now he brushes his hair with everything brush-like, including the broom and the nailbrush. When he saw me shaving my legs this morning, he tried to help using the spoon he was holding!
> (Karmiloff-Smith 1994: 185)

This is a wonderful example of a child being inducted into the practices of his mother. He watches what she does and then copies it. In doing this he has been able to compare objects and make a category of 'brush' and then selected and used other types of brush in order to do what his mother has done. He has also generalised the concept of 'scraper' when he sees his mother shaving her legs (which must look like scraping them) and uses the spoon in his hand as a scraper.

In considering mediation we need to think about three other concepts which are internalisation, participation and memory. Let us start with *internalisation* because, although we haven't yet used the term, we have already encountered the idea. You will remember that Vygotsky talked about how the child was moved from coming to understand though sharing with an adult or *more expert learner* (interpsychological) to responding on her own (intrapsychological). At the heart of this is the process of internalisation. It is as though the child takes into her own consciousness the learning that has taken place. So the child becomes aware of what has been learned. Internalisation must be seen in the context of social interaction and in terms of the system of meanings (or the systems of signs and symbols, also called *semiotic* systems), which mediate social functioning. Read about Rehana and her birthday party to learn more about internalisation.

> Four-year-old Rehana has had four years of being drawn into the culture of her home and six months of being drawn into the culture of her nursery

class. She was drawn into the culture of her home by her interactions with her parents and older siblings and inducted into the things that are part of her everyday home life. She understands and speaks Sylheti. She loves the curries and rice her mother serves every day. She knows lots of songs in Bengali. She was drawn into the culture of her nursery class through her interactions with her teacher and her peers: drawn into the things that are part of her weekday nursery environment. She is beginning to speak English and understands it easily. She loves listening to stories with her friends. She is starting to be able to write some words in English. Last week she stayed for school dinner and ate in the classroom with the other children.

Today is her birthday. Her family comes from Bangladesh but she was born in London and has lived there for her whole life. She goes to a nursery in the East End and she is beginning to be able to communicate effectively in both English and Sylheti. For her fourth birthday her mother has said she can have a birthday party and can invite all her cousins and some of her friends from school. From her experience of going to other birthday parties she has requested a birthday cake and her mum has bought one from Marks and Spencer. There are four candles on the cake. Rehana is enjoying every moment of this special day. Her mother invited the children from her class to sing happy birthday to her and her cousins have given her a beautiful new sparkly top to wear on this special day. Her friends from school have given her presents too.

Rehana is now at the centre of the activity around her birthday. She is a full and independent member of the culture of English birthdays. She was inducted into this through what she saw and heard and participated in when other children in her group had birthdays which were celebrated in the class or when she was invited to go to the homes of her friends for these parties. She knew to ask for a birthday cake: she knew there must be the correct number of candles on the cake and she knew that for it to be a party she wanted to invite friends from school. She also wanted a special new top to wear on this special day. She came to be able to do this first through adults drawing her from the periphery into the centre and was then able to sustain her place at the centre by no longer being dependent on adult mediation. But she also internalised her knowledge: this is demonstrated by her knowing what would make her birthday party acceptable to her peers and by knowing what to ask for to make this happen.

We have been talking here about how children become inducted into communities of practice and perhaps need to explain a little more about what this means and why it is important. Communities of practice identify themselves as a group according to the things about them that bind them together. This could be their values, their religion, their feelings, their concerns – any set of principles and behaviours to which they adhere and which they have developed through their interactions with one another. They could identify themselves as 'good mothers' or 'concerned educators' or 'faithful husbands' or 'non-drinkers' or 'orchestral players' or 'conceptual artists' or anything else they choose. What we are saying is that they develop a higher order psychological function, which we call 'an *identity*'. The young learner could be inducted into the roles and rules and practices of the community of practice of the classroom but also into the community of practice of the playground or into the community of practice of children who go to Saturday school. They do this in different ways, sometimes by using the observable behaviour of members of the community as role models or through dialogue and discussion or through joining in with the activities and using the tools specific to each community. Often the adults involved actively induct the children into the ways of the community as we will see when we start to examine things like guided participation. None of this is to suggest that children all become the same as a member of their community. Each retains her own identity. Each still brings her own history, cultural habitus, expectations, feelings and needs.

Participation is, in fact, not a term used by Vygotsky himself but one introduced by those influenced by his work and trying to apply it to today's societies. We often use the term to describe what happens when individuals join in with others during an activity or an experience. Vygotsky, as you will remember, spoke of social and cultural and historical influences on the development of individuals. Some of those who have written about his work emphasise that although his emphasis on the social and cultural was so strong this did not mean that he denied the existence or importance of individual development. Matusov (1998) distinguished between Vygotsky's internalisation model and the participation model and saw them as two different views of cognitive development but with each contributing to a better understanding in a truly dialogic approach. The reason for telling you this is to introduce you to some of the thoughts of Gordon Wells (1999). He has been very influenced by the work of Vygotsky and holds a deeply social view of learning and development. To illustrate his participation model he talks of dancing as a cultural activity. A novice dancer takes a few steps, guided perhaps by a partner, and certainly by the rhythm of the music. But the novice soon begins to get a feel for the dance and is soon able to participate as a full partner, sometimes following and sometimes leading. Wells says there has been no internalisation since no knowledge has passed from expert to novice. Rather, they move in the dance together. The whole activity is so structured that the novice is able to construct the organising cognitive frameworks for herself. I am not sure this is true, being someone who has failed to learn to dance or to ski or to play tennis effectively. Clearly this cannot be a universal model but it is an interesting one to consider.

It is, however, directly relevant to the work done by Barbara Rogoff (1990), who has worked with many different communities, looking at the ways in which infants and young children were inducted into the practices of their communities. The concept she prefers is that of *guided participation*, where the inexperienced or novice learner is alongside the expert in the practices of daily life. Her examples include things like children learning to cook or clean or bake or sew or make things alongside others in her community. We will return to this later.

Memory

Vygotsky was very interested in *memory* – which in effect, means the ability to think about something that has already happened. He conducted various experiments to see just how young children were able to use internalised concepts or memory (for him the terms were synonymous) in order to solve problems.

One of these experiments is known as the toy piano experiment. Here children were asked to associate a picture with a key on the toy piano. The pictures were of everyday objects – an apple, an envelope, and so on. The researchers wanted to see if the children could remember, after a number of turns, which picture went with which key. The question they were asking was this: does the picture of an object (an external stimulus) remind them of the associated key. The youngest children struggled with this. Vygotsky concluded that these children – even those who had some grasp of the relationship – were operating with what he called 'naïve psychology'. A more interesting experiment is one where he and Luria asked children to invent something in the form of a pictorial or symbolic label to help them remember the names of numbers. The purpose was to know how many objects were inside a container without having to open the container and count the objects. Vygotsky noted that this experiment gave him the opportunity to trace the

> very moment of transition, the moment of inventing written language, and second, to immediately discover the deep changes that occur when a child makes the transformation from unmediated remembering to mediated remembering.
>
> (1997: 252)

This is important and it may take you a little while to realise the differences being illustrated by the 'toy piano' and the 'labelling objects' experiments. In the first one the child was using a tool given to them by someone else: they had no ownership of it and it may not have had any significance for them. In other words it may not have been able to serve as a cultural tool. In the second experiment the children were making their own cultural tools, and by now you know well how important that is. Overleaf, just to entertain you, are some labels for tins of objects designed by Hannah when she was about six years old (Figure 2.5). She could easily remember what each label represented.

Memory is a concept you will be familiar with from your everyday experience. Vygotsky talked about the close relationship between external social processes (how others help the learner make sense of something) and internal psychological ones (how the learner becomes able to reflect on things no longer present). We will use an aspect of memory to help illustrate what he meant – you have already come across a good example earlier in this chapter. Do you remember the example of Xian learning a mnemonic device to help him remember the names of the notes on the lines of the treble clef? Let me remind

Figure 2.5 Hannah's labels

you of it. The notes on the treble clef are EGBDF, and Xian's sister taught him the mnemonic '**E**very **G**ood **B**oy **D**eserves **F**ood' – a phrase where each word begins with a letter from the list to be remembered. In all cultures mnemonic and other devices have been developed to help memory, and children in each culture are inducted into these. As children learn these culturally mediated ways of remembering they may have to give up on the individual devices they have developed – things like repeating things, learning them off by heart, and so forth. What seems to happen is that the culturally learned mnemonic devices for remembering replace the earlier idiosyncratic ones. (The labels invented by Hannah are examples of idiosyncratic ones. You will be relieved to know that she no longer has to resort to using this.) The culturally learned devices become internalised and then take over much of the child's remembering and recalling and become integrated with other skills like the use of concepts, storytelling and inference.

Consider four-year-old Jacques setting the table for lunch each day. He knows he needs a plate for himself, a plate for his mum and a plate for his dad; a knife and fork and spoon for each and a glass. Every day for weeks he repeats the same ritual. One plate, back to the dresser to fetch another, back again to fetch a third. Then back to fetch one knife and so on. In all he makes several short journeys to complete this small task. He has developed a physical process to ensure he gets what he needs but it is cumbersome. One day his mum says to him, 'If you carry all three plates at once it is quicker. Look.' And she demonstrates. So for the next week he manages three plates at once but still goes back and forth for the cutlery and the glasses. One day his mum gives him a plastic tray and suggests he use that to help him in this task. This is a cultural tool – something people in his society developed over time in order to help them carry several things at once. Jacques loves his tray and within a few weeks cuts the time it takes him to set the table in half. The use of the cultural tool allows him, once he has internalised how it will help him, to give up his laborious one-to-one correspondence

The tool Jacques uses in this example is a physical one and you need to remind yourself that most of the cultural tools we use are not. Mediation is something central to Vygotsky's thinking. In his own words he said,

> It is through the mediation of others, through the mediation of the adult that the child undertakes activities. Absolutely everything in the behaviour of the child is merged and rooted in social relations. Thus, the child's relations with reality are from the start social relations, so that the newborn baby could be said to be in the highest degree a social being.
> (Vygotsky 1932)

More on the importance of cultural tools

It is essential for us to know what Vygotsky meant by the term cultural tools and why they are so important to an understanding of his ideas and his work. Although you have already been introduced to these ideas it is worth repeating them here as a reminder. Cultural tools are devices humans use for mastering their thinking and problem-solving. They are not natural but artificial (by which we mean created by humans) and they have come about through social rather than individual actions. Among the things that Vygotsky defined as cultural tools are these: language; systems of counting; mnemonic devices; symbols including algebraic and musical symbols; works of art; writing; diagrams; maps; road signs; and so on. Can you see how each of these has come about through the efforts of people working in groups or societies and have come about as ways of refining thinking and helping solve problems?

- We have developed a system of symbols to represent numbers. This enables us to use a kind of shorthand to represent our thinking. So if we need to work out how many objects we have if we have 10 groups of 5 objects we can express this as $10 \times 5 = 50$ and don't have to lay out 10 groups with 5 objects in each.
- If we need to go from our own home to another place this is made simpler if we have a representational and diagrammatic plan to help us. So we use a map.
- Our culture has developed a system of road signs in order to ensure that drivers and cyclists and pedestrians can travel more safely by knowing what is ahead of them, what is permissible and what not.

Cultural tools are the products of human cultural and historical activity. Pea (1993) says that these tools literally carry intelligence in them, in that they represent some individual's or some community's decision that the means thus offered would be reified, made stable, as a quasi permanent form, for the use of others.

(Pea 1993)

He goes on to say that as the tools become so familiar as to be almost invisible it gets harder to see them 'carrying' intelligence. He says that what we see is that intelligence lies with the person who is using the tools. Cole (1996) suggests that cultural tools should be considered a sub-category of the over-arching notion of *artefact* – where artefacts are defined as objects created by man (*sic*). People and objects can both act as mediating artefacts.

In all cultures throughout the world people have developed ways of *representing* their thoughts and feelings through using symbolic means like writing, painting, music and dance. Vygotsky was insistent that humans become aware of their own thoughts through and with these tools. The question is often asked 'Can you think without language?' and although responses to this differ it seems clear that most of us believe that we need some additional tool (drawing, painting, music, symbols, language) in order to make clear to ourselves (which is how we might define 'thinking') what we are thinking or contemplating. Vygotsky would argue the following:

1   The individual is an active agent in the process.
2   Everything takes place within a context where the individual uses the tools which are available at that time and in that place.

We spoke earlier about mnemonic devices being used as early cultural tools. Vygotsky used the now famous example of when a knot is tied in a handkerchief as a reminder to do something. This, he argues, is an external agent of remembering. The process of remembering is triggered and reconstructed by having this external symbol. This, for him, marks a significant shift in revealing how human beings can be in control of their future remembering. We will return to this when we look at his thoughts on language.

We can summarise Vygotsky's thoughts on cultural tools as follows:

- When a tool is developed it allows for the development of several new functions connected with the use of the tool and its control.
- When a tool is developed it allows several natural processes to die out since the tool now accomplishes the work done by these processes. This means that thinking becomes more efficient, more complex, and quicker.
- The whole structure of behaviour is changed in the same way that the development of material tools (hammers, computers for example) changes the whole structure of physical or labour tasks.

To illustrate some of these ideas here are some examples, drawn from the work of Kenner (2004a). In these examples you can see how children are inducted into the ideas and customs of their culture through interaction with others and through the use of cultural tools. In her book *Becoming Biliterate: Young Children Learning Different Writing Systems* Kenner set out to illustrate the complex knowledge that young bilingual children have about their own written languages. Her interest was primarily to show how these young children, through teaching their peers about their writing systems, revealed the extremely high-level cognitive functions through the psychological tool of written language. Her analysis was not a Vygotskian one but it is revealing to apply such an analysis to this work.

We start with looking at Ming. He, like all the other children in the study, is six years old. In one of the peer teaching sessions he was trying to teach his friend Amina how to write the Chinese symbol for the number seven. Some of her attempts looked too much like the number four. Kenner says

> Ming was concerned that Amina might be seeing the Chinese symbol from an English perspective, so he corrected her. 'That's a four! That's wrong'.
> (Kenner 2004a: 112)

What can we learn from this? Ming has learned all he knows about Chinese symbols and how they are written and what they mean through interactions with expert users of Chinese in his family and community. But he has also been inducted into the conventions of the English written system through his interactions with his peers and their teachers. Faced with teaching Amina, who has no knowledge of Chinese symbols, he solves the problem of what is wrong with her attempt at writing the symbol for seven by comparing it with something he knows that she knows – the English numerical system. He is using the cultural tools of graphics and numerical systems and spoken language to vocalise the problem.

Earlier in the book there is a wonderful example of Selina, also a Chinese speaker, trying to teach her best friend Ruby how to write the complex character for the concept of 'tomorrow'. Selina had learned how to do this at her Chinese school and the character involved making eight strokes in sequence. Ruby tried and tried but could not manage it. In fact, her attempts were so dismal that Selina rubbed them out and made her start again. Selina was not able to give Ruby very much oral help, other than telling her that it was not right. She clearly expected Ruby to be able to look at her attempt, compare it with the correct version and get it right. This was a cultural tool available to Selina through her experiences but not available to Ruby. Over time, however, she realised that Ruby actually needed explicit verbal help to manage the task so she started to say things to her like 'not like a square' which had the effect of indicating to Ruby that she needed to learn to pay attention to the exact shapes and features of each stroke. Kenner tells us that for Selina, each stroke of the character carried meaning and significance. She had learned, from Chinese school, how each stroke related to each other stroke. Over time Ruby began to make self-critical comments like 'That bit was too long'. So Ruby, through her interactions with a more experienced Chinese-character writer, was being inducted into the cultural tools that could facilitate her learning of how to do this (Kenner 2004a: 78–9).

One more example, this time drawn from the work of Duranti *et al.*, in Gregory (2004). They looked at the schooling experiences of children in a Samoan community and how this changed as Samoan children were brought to America. Missionaries to Samoa took with them aspects of Western culture and Christianity when they tried to introduce literacy as part of their mission. The authors tell us that Samoan infants were invariably carried on the hips and backs of their older siblings and carried in this way to church. In the schools set up by the missionaries some initial literacy instruction had been carried out through what was (and still is) known as the Pi Tautau. This is a poster which displays the Samoan alphabet with Roman and Arabic numerals at the bottom. Each letter is accompanied by a picture of an object beginning with that letter. Children were expected to sit cross-legged on the floor with the other children, while the teacher – sitting on a chair – pointed to one picture at a time – left to right – while the children recited the letter and the name of the image and then the name of the letter alone. Many of the images were of things not familiar to these children. They had probably never seen a chicken or a car or a rabbit and would almost certainly have never heard of Herod! This way of teaching did little to build on the culture and experiences of the children yet when families emigrated to America they brought with them aspects of this teaching. The Pi Tautau was still a reflection of strange and unfamiliar objects but in this new and often hostile culture it carried with it strong memories of the past, of links with ancestors and a reminder of the powerful psychological tool of the language of the families.

Children in Samoa spoke Samoan. Children transplanted to California now have a rudimentary knowledge of Samoan and some of their teachers know even less of Samoan than they do. So here the children are in the position of being more expert about Samoan language than their teachers. There is much language switching (from English to Samoan and back) in the research described, and children are sometimes heard correcting their teachers about things like pronunciation. In their analysis of this the researchers suggest that one of the main functions of maintaining first or community languages is to retain cultural identity and heritage. Here we see the powerful impact of society and community in learning and the powerful effect of cultural tools, developed within societies and communities on learning but also on identity.

Looking back, looking ahead

In this chapter we have said that when Vygotsky talked of mediation he was thinking about the use of communicable systems (by which he meant the ways in which ideas and thoughts could be communicated by one person to another or to groups of others) both for representing reality and for acting on it. He saw this as the basis of all cognition.

For Vygotsky the role of others in learning was essential and by others he meant not only adults but also, crucially, other children. He believed that during socialisation (interacting with others) the child was inducted or drawn into the culture and then internalised the means of being part of that culture through the very fact of her common participation in activities with others. So sharing something with another person allows the child to take the first steps in becoming a member of the shared culture of that interaction. We have also looked in some detail at cultural tools and seen how these may be material or communicable systems and are what shape the development of thinking. So the child is born into a culture and becomes a full member of that culture through making meaning of all aspects of that culture – the practices and beliefs and values. The child does this through using the communicable systems as tools which allow the child's thinking to change.

Vygotsky said that

> The inclusion of a tool in the process of behaviour (a) introduces several new functions connected with the use of the given tool and with its control; (b) abolishes and makes unnecessary several natural processes whose work is accomplished by the tool; and alters the course and individual features (the intensity, duration, sequence, etc.) of all the mental processes that enter into the composition of the instrumental act, replacing some functions with others (i.e. it re-creates and reorganizes the whole structure of behaviour just as a technical tool re-creates the whole structure of labor operations).
>
> (Vygotsky 1981: 139–40)

In the next chapter we will start to think in more detail about the importance of culture and context.

Glossary

Word or phrase	What it means	Why it is significant
artefact	An object or objects created by people within groups or cultures.	Artefacts include cultural tools like objects or systems.
collaborative activity	This is something in which those involved have to share and negotiate.	Since all learning is social the more collaborative activities we offer the more opportunities there are for sharing and negotiating.

communicable systems	Language is a communicable system and one of the ways we have found of sharing ideas.	So much of learning involves communication that we need to understand as much as possible about the systems that allow this.
cultural tools	See page 18.	
culture	See page 18.	
guided participation	A term used by Barbara Rogoff to explain the learning that takes place through adults and children being together in real-life situations.	This is important as one of the ways in which children can be moved from cognitive dependence to cognitive independence.
higher order mental functions	These are things like being able to classify, order, generalise, compare and so on.	We will work towards helping children be able to develop these more abstract concepts.
historical	An everyday word meaning a study of the past.	Its significance for us is that we need to know as much as possible about what the child already knows and can do and about what the child has experienced.
identity	An everyday word with complex meanings but all related to self-concept.	Children develop a sense of their identity as they make sense of who they are and where they are placed and how they are perceived by others.
instrumental	For Vygotsky this meant the use of cultural tools to bring about cognitive changes.	It is important to understand the concept rather than the word.
internalisation	One of the most important of Vygotsky's ideas, it means something going within and not being obvious to others.	Internalisation marks the beginning of the process of children being able to deal with concepts without having an object or situation to refer to.

interpsychological	This means something shared between the child and someone else.	It is important to understand the concept rather than the word.
intrapsychological	This means something that is within the child – that has been internalised.	It is important to understand the concept rather than the word.
mediation	A key concept to grasp, this refers to the use of cultural tools made by people to interpret and explain the world.	Cannot be summarised adequately here but it is something you must ensure you understand.
memory	An everyday word which means to be able to recall something experienced before.	Memory is a vital tool which allows learners to be able to handle abstract ideas without having to have the real objects to hand.
mnemonic	A device to assist memory.	A tool to assist remembering something which later becomes internalised and no longer needed.
more expert other	Vygotsky insisted that not only adults could take learning forward. A child with more experience or knowledge of the task at hand could do so. Someone with more experience is referred to in some of his work as a more expert other.	The concept is important because it reminds us that children learn from all their encounters and offers us ideas about how we can use other children to support the learning of novices and to teach them.
participation	Means to join in or take part.	See page 20.
psychobiological	Means relating to the emotions and also to the links between the natural, the social, the cultural and the environmental.	

representing	An everyday word which means 'stand for' or, literally, re-present or present again.	It is important in how children become able to express their thoughts and ideas. They can represent objects or thoughts through writing or drawing or music or dance.
semiotic	This word is one you should learn since you are likely to encounter it again in your reading. It means the study of systems of signs or symbols.	Since most of the school learning children need involves the use of symbols, knowing something about semiotics is essential for all those working with children.
sign	A sign is something that stands for or represents an object or an idea. A triangular road sign stands for danger.	Part of the system of semiotics, so it is essential to understand.
symbol	A symbol is something that stands for or represents something else. The symbol for email is known to you. ✉	Part of the system of semiotics, so it is essential to understand.
symbolic	One thing representing another. Young children, in pretend play, use one thing to stand for another.	Essential to understand this since it is how children are able to come to use the symbolic cultural tools of language, mathematics, music and so on.

Chapter 3

More on culture, context and tools

In this chapter we examine more deeply what Vygotsky and his followers thought about culture, and explore its relevance for us, as those working with or caring for children and young people. We are used to being told that we must pay close attention to what the child has already learned at home, in the family, in the local community and perhaps during previous years of formal or informal education and care. We are less used to thinking about this in terms of culture. So understanding exactly what Vygotsky meant by the term 'cultural' is essential if we are to understand his concern with how knowledge is passed on from generation to generation.

Development and culture

To ensure that we have a shared understanding it is important to define some terms. We will start with *development*. You might want to think about what this means to you and you might also want to consider how helpful the word is to you in understanding human behaviour and progress. You almost certainly use the word often in your ordinary life, talking about child development, perhaps. A common-sense definition would say that development is the sequence of physical, social and intellectual changes the human organism (if we are thinking about human development) undergoes from the moment of conception until the finality of death. So development goes from conception through birth, through infancy and into childhood, through adolescence into adulthood and old age. We are thinking of something like Shakespeare's 'seven ages of man'. So the word development describes changes. It does not explain how and why changes take place, nor whether progress takes place in stages or not, nor what the actual process of change might be. You will notice that the definition does not mention culture.

Let us start by repeating an earlier definition of culture which you can then compare with the one I am offering you to consider now. We said earlier that culture could be defined as the ways in which groups of people pass on beliefs and values and the products of human work and thought. Here is another definition, this time that of D'Andrade (1996) who says that *culture is the socially inherited body of past human accomplishments that serves as the resources for the current life of a social group*. Conventionally this social group is thought of as the inhabitants of a country or region. It is worth reading through this definition again but it is wordy and complex and perhaps underlining the key words would be helpful. For me the key words are 'socially', 'inherited, 'body', human accomplishments' and 'resources'. The definition, for all its brevity, sums up the essence of culture. People, in groups, create ideas and objects that in themselves then change the ideas and the things and this goes on and on. Michael Cole (2006) summarises this as follows:

> A new tool is developed. This leads to being able to grow more food. As a result brain size increases and the skill of running develops: this, perhaps, leads to more food and better shelter and a longer life. This, in its turn, leads to larger social groups of those with bigger and more complex brains … and so it goes. [Author's interpretation]

The 'accomplishments' that D'Andrade talks of may be material things that humans make – things like pots or baskets or computers or cars or tables or iPods – or they may be conceptual things like religious beliefs, the laws of thermodynamics, the grammar of languages and so on. The material and the conceptual come together in cultural practices, ways of doing things or beliefs and values. This means that the material and conceptual combine to bring out what come to be regarded as the usual ways of doing things within a group, remembering that this is governed by material resources, modes of behaviour and beliefs. Here are some examples to illustrate this:

> In a mountainous region of Italy semolina is grown. It is thus plentiful and affordable. As a result many local dishes have developed, based on semolina.
>
> In South Africa, as in most other countries, there is the urge for people to make music and in the absence of Western musical instruments people developed instruments of their own from natural and found objects. They made drums and thumb pianos and marimbas.

Living in a culture we become so much part of it that we often don't think about what it is that makes us who we are within that culture. It is often only when people lose their culture, for one reason or another, that they become more able to describe what makes their culture what it is.

Losing a culture: on exile

The experiences of people who are in exile from their home countries are interesting and relevant in that they illustrate well what makes culture such a powerful presence in all our lives.

The South African judge, Albie Sachs, in a recent lecture in London, talked about his experience of being an exile from his beloved South Africa. After being imprisoned and tortured for his beliefs he agreed to take an 'exit permit' from that country and come to the United Kingdom. The exit permit meant that he could not return to his home country. He spoke English and was not identifiable as different through the colour of his skin, yet he found himself in a place where much was alien to him and where he struggled (and believed he failed) to become part of the new culture. He talked of a sense of being apart despite people's efforts to welcome him. He studied and lived here for many years, yet when an opportunity came to go and live in Mozambique (closer to South Africa) he grabbed it and found many things were better for him there because the culture was so much closer to the one he had left.

The great Brazilian educator, Paolo Freire, was in exile in a number of countries for almost twenty years. He, like Sachs, was in exile because of his political views and his determination to deal with poverty, illiteracy and oppression. In an interview with Antonio Faundez he spoke of his growing awareness of the importance of his Brazilian culture during his exile. He talked about how, through experiencing a different everyday life, he learned to become part of this everyday life. He felt integrated into it and he believed he learned what he called 'the rules of the games'. But he also had to learn about differences and how to live with them and he talked about how some of the things he had to learn he could never really internalise. One of these was the attitude of people in his new cultures (in Europe and the United States) to the human body and how vastly different this was from the attitude to the body in Brazil. He said:

> It is the human body, young or old, fat or thin, of whatever colour, the conscious body, that looks at the stars. It is the body that writes. It is the body that speaks. It is the body that fights. It is the body that loves and hates. It is the body that suffers. It is the body that dies. It is the body that lives! It has not been unusual for me to put my hand affectionately on someone's shoulder only to find my hand suddenly in mid-air, while the body I wanted to touch shrunk away refusing contact with mine.
>
> (Freire and Macedo 2001: 204)

Later, in the same interview he talked of how the most serious problem that faces someone uprooted from their own culture is that they have to constantly stand back from aspects of everyday life which are not familiar to them. He says it is as though the person is constantly on guard. It is clear that for him culture is about everything that makes up the life of a group – the gestures and the words, the relationships with people and the relationships with things. Learning to live in a new culture may be about learning a different language, eating in a different way, becoming able to accept other values.

The importance of this for those of you who work with children should be evident. In almost every group or setting there will be children who may have parents who are exiles or, if not exiles, are still living in a country with a culture that is new and unfamiliar. Understanding something of what it means to leave your culture behind as you have to adapt to a new one is extremely important if we are to ease these children into this, their new culture.

Developmental niches

This was not a term used by Vygotsky and was developed long after his death. It is, however, very useful to us in trying to understand the role of culture in development. The term means *where any child is situated within an always complex set of relations – social, cultural and ecological – that form the child's developmental environment*. In simple terms it means things like the following:

- *where the child lives* and *who* the child interacts with in his or her daily life;
- *the ways in which the child is being reared and socialised* into the conventions of her family and community;
- the psychological *characteristics of the child's parents* and especially those that impinge on how the child is being brought up, what the expectations of the parents are and so on.

Those of you familiar with the work of Bronfenbrenner will recognise something of his model which is often conceived of as a series of concentric circles (Figure 3.1). In this model the child is at the centre and around the child is a *microsystem* made up of the home in which are the child, parents and, possibly, siblings; the religious setting in which are the child, peers and adults; the school or setting, in which are the child, educators and peers; and the neighbourhood, in which are the child, adults and peers. The first concentric circle describes the *mesosystem*, which defines the interactions between home, school, neighbourhood and religious settings. Next is the *exosystem*, describing the impact (real or potential) of local industry, parents' workplaces, local government, mass media and school or setting management committee. Finally, and most remote from the child, are the *macrosystems*, which define the dominant beliefs and ideologies operating for that child and her family. Into this come things like laws.

Here are some case studies to help you understand this.

> Four-year-old Jeremiah has just started in the reception class in the school which his brother and sister attend. His parents are keen that he attend a Jewish day school because they want him to have the same sort of education his father had. The family lives in a large house in a middle-class area of a city. Father is a lawyer and mother a university lecturer. The children all learn to play musical instruments and their mother supervises their daily practice and attends all their lessons. The children's homework is also supervised and mother is quick to turn up at school if something goes wrong. The parents are very interested in school success and the children are rewarded when they

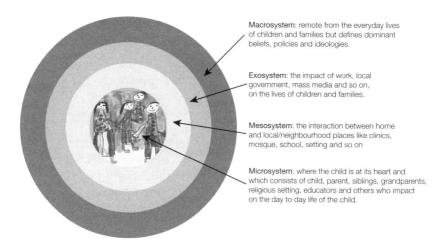

Figure 3.1 Bronfenbrenner's ecological model

do well in tests or exams. The family approves of the present government which is keen to restrict immigration and reward private enterprise.

Jeremiah's microsystem consists of him and his siblings and parents; the synagogue and those who attend it; the Jewish day school and the teachers and children there; and the local neighbourhood, which includes his grandparents, aunts, uncles and cousins. The interactions between aspects of his microsystem are regular and predictable: there are few contradictions or difficulties. Most of the people the family knows attend the same schools and the same synagogue. Similarly, the parents, living middle-class lives and working as professionals, encounter other people like them and are little affected by other aspects of the exosystem. The family's happiness with the government and their policies, their religion and its policies, indicate their contentment with the macrosystem.

Four-year-old Shah Jahan does not go to school. He lives with his parents in a hut in the countryside in a desert-like area of Rajasthan. There are three other children in his family and all of them work in the fields alongside their mum. They are supposed to go to school but it is far away and the family feels it would be better for them all if the children were kept close to the family and safe from the marauding gangs said to be in the area. Nonetheless the family is keen that the children learn and the oldest daughter of the family in the next hut comes each evening to spend an hour or two teaching the children. They are learning to read and can all write. Because they help their father take goods to market they are all adept at calculating and handling money. Their father reads to them every evening (his father taught him to read) and so they know many stories and re-tell them to one another and act them out with figures they make from things they find in the environment. Shah Jahan loves to draw and paint and has learned to make colours by crushing berries and petals and leaves. His grandmother showed him how to do this. The family do not like their current government because they feel that although the country is getting richer, they appear to be getting poorer. The father often says that India is a country of extremes: those getting richer and richer at the expense of those getting poorer and poorer.

Shah Jahan's developmental niche is more complex. He lives with his family in the countryside and has relationships with family and neighbours. He does not go to school nor does he go to worship anywhere. The family is too busy making a living and surviving. Yet they understand the importance of education and do what they can to ensure their children have access to learning to read and write. Aspects of the exosystem are very important in their lives as you can see from the children going with their father to market to sell the produce and by so doing are learning about money and about counting. The traditions of the community are being passed on from one generation to another as we see with Shah Jahan painting using natural colours and the children acting out stories with figures they make. The impact of the macrosystem on this family is great and negative. They are aware of their unending poverty in light of the growing wealth of others in their country.

When Rita decided to have a child she was certain about how she wanted this to happen. She had read articles about how the foetus can hear and was determined that her new child should be exposed to what she called 'good music' before birth. So, even though she was not very fond of classical music, she bought some CDs of music by Mozart and ensured that she spent an hour each afternoon of her pregnancy listening to these. She was also determined that the baby should be born at home and spent months preparing the room for the birth. She wanted a birthing partner and her friend volunteered to do this. The new baby was called Amber and slept in a rush basket at the foot of her parents' bed. Rita was determined that the child should never be distressed so at the first whimper she would pick up the child and feed or comfort her. It is up to you to decide how you think this little girl grew up.

Here you can see how the macrosystem, in terms of the values taken on by the mother and received by her through the media, influenced the child even before birth. So culture has an impact from before birth and continues throughout life.

If you think about the children you know, you will realise the complexities embedded in all their lives in terms of all the various matters, close by and remote, that have an impact on their lives. Cole believes that culture is the specific medium of human life, through which the interactions between biology and the child's experiences with the environment are mediated.

The role of biology

Vygotsky recognised that psychological phenomena, while being organised by cultural processes and cultural tools, also involve *biological* processes. If you think of the role of biology in the life of an infant and in the life of a four-year-old you will realise that biology plays a far more dominant role in the life of the infant than in the life of the child. This is because social experiences begin to take over the lives of human beings and, as they do so, the influence of the biological recedes. The educators in the famous *asili nidi* (crèches) for infants and toddlers in Reggio Emilia recognise this fact and reflect it in their practice. The *routines of the day*, related to biological need, dominate in the early months of life but through socialisation take up less and less of the time as social processes, interactions and games come to predominate. Early in life naturally determined behaviours predominate, governed by instincts and hormones, and these include smiling, grasping, crying, reaching, persistence and so on. It takes no leap of imagination to see how early in life these become social responses as others in the environment respond to them.

On a London tube train an infant, probably about 12 months old, was sitting in her buggy watching everything that happened. She listened intently when announcements were made and her eyes followed the moving text telling passengers the destination of the train. But when a young man came and sat opposite her what happened was fascinating, entertaining, and a perfect example of early socialisation. The young man smiled at her and she smiled back and then stuck out her tongue. He copied her and then winked at her. Winking back was something she couldn't work out how to do so, instead, she flicked her fingers past her eyelid and watched his response. He winked again and this time she covered both eyes with her hands and then, dramatically, removed them. She was clearly inviting him to engage in a peekaboo game, which he did. After a while she was distracted by a man further down the carriage, who was taking no notice of her at all but engaged in deep and earnest conversation with the young woman beside him. Throughout the conversation, he nodded from time to time. The little girl watched intently, and when he stopped nodding, she started nodding. By this time other people in the carriage became aware of the interactions and watched, smiling. Just then a young Spanish couple with a small child, roughly the same age as our little girl, got on the train and stood beside the child's pram. The little girls spotted one another and smiled, at first tentatively and then full gummy smiles of delight. Over a few minutes their interaction moved on to touching one another's fingers, trying to reach one another's hair, exchanging streams of speech-like sounds and eventually waving goodbye to one another, encouraged by the parents. A proto relationship and conversation.

The early behaviours of smiling and grasping, among others, are simple, possibly unconscious, and often involuntary responses. Vygotsky referred to these behaviours as elementary or *lower processes*. He saw that the infant, equipped with only these lower processes, is tied to the physical world and responds to events that affect her directly, but is not yet able to think about the world or understand it. Vygotsky talked of the infant having immediate blind reactions to stimuli. To become fully human we have to develop higher mental processes which then mediate between us and the world. In their writing Vygotsky and Luria say that what has to happen is a significant cultural reconstruction so that the young child is able to move from this early stage of primitive perceptions to being able to adapt to the external world.

We are back to the importance of others in both creating cultural tools and inducting less experienced learners into using them.

Money as a cultural tool

We are going to take a look at a cultural tool which seems almost universal in the sense that it appears, in some form or other, in most of the cultures of the world. The cultural tool we are considering is money and the inspiration for this is the work of Michael Cole, who used it as one of his examples in a recent lecture (2003). You may think that money originated only within a system of barter, in which something needed by one group could be supplied by another group in exchange for something the latter group needed. You will have read accounts of people exchanging one pig for three bags of potatoes, or a knitted sweater for some cheese, or a drum for a bag of salt and so on. Systems of barter and exchange have developed in all cultures. Alongside this a system of banking appears to have been developed in some cultures, which needed places where valuables could be kept safely. Some time later a system of receipts or written records of what was deposited in the bank was developed.

The first systems of money were in the form of precious metals that could be weighed. Weighing them allowed for some comparison so that more weight represented a more precious resource. It was only over time that a system of money involving counting was developed. Primitive forms of money were made up of units of items which shared the same characteristics and could easily be counted – cowrie shells, iron nails, sword blades and so on. A little while later some cultures started to produce coins but these coins were easy to counterfeit and were often made of base metals which did not allow for them to be used in the purchase of large or scarce and precious resources. When coins were first minted from precious metals they were sometimes inscribed or stamped in order to show they were genuine. Money came to be a means of payment. Paper money developed later and certainly not universally.

What this meant was that countable, coin-based systems developed across the world, coins being stamped or inscribed to show their pedigree. A would-be purchaser could take 100 of these coins to a trader in order to buy an item. After a while it became apparent that carrying 100 coins was inconvenient and new coins were minted in different denominations: ten larger 10-denomination coins were the equivalent of 100 small coins; and two even larger 50-denomination coins were the equivalent of 100 small coins. But you know all of this. It is the stuff of your everyday life. Money became both a unit of account and a common measure. The importance of this was that people could compare prices, know the worth of an item, and ensure that what they handed over was exactly the same as what some other person handed over.

The invention of coins (and, later, of notes) allowed all sorts of transactions which had not been possible before. Can you think what these might be? One of the things that became possible was the system of loans. If you did not have enough money for something you needed, someone might be kind enough to lend you the money – or, perhaps, some of the money. And from that arose a system of debts and interest and mortgages, and eventually the stock market, and so on.

Cole tells us that the word 'money' comes from the name of a Roman goddess, Moneta – the queen of the gods, also known as Juno. But it appears that *Moneta* was a translation of the Greek word *Mnemosyne*, who was goddess of memory and mother of the Muses. *Moneta* was derived from the Latin word *moneio*, which means, among other things, 'to remind, put in mind of, bring to one's recollection'. How fascinating that the word 'money' shares a root with the Latin word for memory.

So money operates both as a cultural tool and as a *material tool*. It operates as a cultural tool because the very use of it has changed thinking and practice and our young children are inducted into the world of exchange and money through their social interactions with others. In our daily lives we use money without thinking about what it represents, but we often see young children struggling to understand how one coin can stand for or represent the same thing as ten other coins. You will be familiar with children asking questions about money or credit cards or cheques or banks or borrowing or lending – all concepts related to money. Young children playing at shops often show a lack of understanding of where money comes from, what change means and who gets paid and for what and by whom. Here is an example to illustrate how children come to understand and use this cultural tool.

> Rinaldo, Charlie and Elinor are playing in the garden. They are all three years old. They have found some pebbles and some pinecones and have set up a shop in the old shed. Rinaldo says he will be the shopkeeper. Charlie wants to know what he has to sell in the shop and Rinaldo says that all the things in his shop are food. Charlie needs more detail and after a while Rinaldo gets a piece of paper and some pens and makes some marks on the paper.
>
> 'These are what I got,' he says. 'Sweets and crisps and … um, ice cream.'
>
> Elinor comes up to them and asks for some sweets. Rinaldo asks her what kind she would like.
>
> 'I will have the chewy kind and pink ones, only. I love pink things.'
>
> Rinaldo fiddles around and then gives her two pinecones. 'Here are your pink sweeties and you have to pay.'
>
> Elinor puts her hand in her pockets and says, 'But I don't have any

money.'

Charlie intervenes and gives her two pebbles, saying, 'These are your monies.'

She gives both to Rinaldo who puts them on the 'counter' of the shop. 'Thanks,' he mutters.

She stands there looking at him. 'I gave you two and I need change.'

'OK,' says Rinaldo and gives her three pebbles.

'Thanks. Bye,' says Elinor.

Charlie shouts, 'No! You can't get three change if you only gave him two. That's not how it works.'

Rinaldo replies, 'She gave me two and I gave her two sweets and this is her change.'

Charlie, exasperated, tried to argue 'But you can't give her three when she only gave you two.'

At that moment one of the adults comes past and asks what is happening. The children explain the situation and the adult immediately understands that at least one of the children is having difficulties with the concept of change. So she goes inside and gets out some of the toy money and shows the children the 1p coins and the 10p coins and tries to explain how the 10p, although it is only one coin, is the equivalent of lots of the 1p coins. The children are baffled, lose concentration and the play breaks down.

But a week later the same children are playing indoors in the shop in the classroom. Elinor has been 'making money' and she gives each of the boys a piece of paper.

'That's pounds,' she explains, and goes on to give them each two lumps of plasticine. 'And that's little money. When I give you a pound you can give me these [she points to the plasticine lumps] for change.'

You can see from this example how the children, familiar with the concepts of money and shopping, are trying to sort out for themselves the meaning of change. The abstract explanation of the adult on the previous occasion failed to help them but Elinor seemed to have made some leap in understanding, demonstrated by the money she had 'made'.

The teacher who observed this later took Elinor to one side to talk to her about the pounds and the small money. Here is a brief account of what happened:

Teacher: You made some pounds and some small money to use in the shop. That was a good idea.
Elinor: My mum sometimes gives me small money to buy something at the shop. She doesn't use small money. She uses paper money or her credit card.
Teacher: Does she ever get change when she uses paper money?
Elinor: Oh yeah! She gives the paper money to the shopkeeper and he gives her lots of coins back.

Teacher:	Why does she get change?
Elinor:	'Cos she paid too much. Anyway, that's what she always says. And she always looks at the money he gives her back and shakes her head. I don't know why.
Teacher:	Does she ever get change when she pays with her credit card?
Elinor:	No! It's not real money. And she never pays for sweets with that. Only clothes and stuff.
Teacher:	Do you think a credit card is the same as money?
Elinor	(laughs): No, you can't fold it.

I love this example because it shows so clearly how hard children work to make sense of the things they encounter as part of their everyday life. Change is clearly getting money back, but quite why is unclear. Big money (notes) can be used to pay for important things like clothes and can be folded. A credit card is even more mysterious but it clearly cannot be folded so it cannot be the same as money.

Many years ago the children in a Year 2 class of a London primary school were asked about their ideas on power. They were asked to rank a group of people in the school according to importance and power, and to give reasons for their responses. What they said was fascinating. The people who they were asked to rank were the following:

1   Children
2   Nursery teacher
3   Nursery nurses
4   Dinner ladies
5   Lollipop person
6   Teaching assistants
7   School keeper
8   Headteacher
9   Secretary
10 Teachers.

Almost universally children were ranked lowest, and highest were either the school keeper or the secretary. When giving their reasons for these responses most of those who chose the secretary as the most powerful person in the school said it was because 'She's got all the money'. When probed it became clear that they believed that all the dinner money went directly to the secretary. Those who had selected the school keeper as the most powerful person in the school said it was because 'He has all the keys'. When asked why children were the least powerful, responses included 'Well, they don't get any money, do they?' or 'They are just kids, like us'. For these children it was clear that money and keys symbolised or represented power. And they could only have arrived at this conclusion through their interactions with others and with their ideas and values.

Signs, symbols and semiotics

In order to understand more about mediation and cultural tools it is important to learn a little about *semiotics*, which is the study of signs. You will remember that we defined the terms symbol and sign in an earlier chapter. We seem, as a species, to be driven by a need to understand the world – to make meaning of it. Gordon Wells, in much of his work, talks of people – and children in particular – as what he calls 'meaning-makers'. By this he is thinking of how hard children work to make sense of the world, and much of this is through the making, use and interpretation of signs. Signs may take many forms. They may take the form of words, images, sounds, flavours, acts or objects, but none of these have any *intrinsic* meaning until we invest them with meaning. Anything can be a sign as long as someone interprets it as 'signifying' or meaning something. So it can refer to or *stand for* something other than itself. We interpret things as signs largely unconsciously by relating them to familiar systems or conventions. It is this meaningful use of signs which is at the heart of semiotics. Some of the most fundamental and important work on semiotics was carried out by Ferdinand de Saussure (1974) early in the twentieth century and he pointed out that there is no rigid or essential relationship between the thing that carries the meaning (which is usually a symbol like a word, for example) and the actual meaning. So the word 'horse' is not a real horse: in English it is the 'word' we have invented to mean horse. In fact the meaning of 'horse' could be carried by any string of letters. In French the letters are c-h-e-v-a-l, but the horse is still a horse. The American philosopher C.S. Pierce, writing at more or less the same time, discussed three types of signs which he called icons, indexes and symbols.

Just for fun you might like to try reading the little story below and answering the questions after the story. The story goes like this:

> This is the story of the Wuggen and the Tor.
> Onz upon a pime a wuggen zonked into the grabbet. Ze was grolling for poft because ze was blongby.
> The wuggen grolled and grolled until ze motte a tor.
> Ze blind to the tor, 'Ik am blongby and grolling for poft. Do yum noff rem ike can gine some poft?'
> 'Kex,' glind ze tor. 'Klom with ne wuggen. Ik have lodz of poft in ni bove.'

Now see if you can answer these questions:

1 Where did the wuggen zonk?
2 What was s/he grolling for?
3 Why was s/he grolling for poft?
4 Who did s/he meet?
5 What on earth was this about?

(Browne 1996: 36)

I have no doubt that you could make sense of that story, although it was written in no recognisable language. But you drew on all your experiences of how written language works and on your experiences of stories. Then, because you, as a meaning-maker, are driven to make sense of print you would have been able to construct something meaningful. The amazing human mind!

We have touched on the importance of symbols in the last example where we saw how young children come to understand how one thing can stand for, represent or symbolise another. For the children in our earlier example keys and money represented power. How the children came to understand that involved mediation, which we looked at earlier in this book. You may want to go back and remind yourself of what we said. Scribner, writing in 1990, tells us that one of the things that made Vygotsky so significant was that he was the first person to appreciate the importance of the social in things, or objects, as well as in people. What Scribner meant was that the world we live in is one made by and for humans, full of material and symbolic objects (signs, knowledge systems and so on), all 'culturally constructed, historical in origin and social in context' (Scribner 1990: 92). All human actions – thinking included – involve the mediation of such objects (i.e. signs and tools). We have thought already about whether it is possible to think without language and may have concluded that some cultural tool or sign is involved in thinking. Since all cultural tools and signs are human constructs it follows that all human actions are social.

The importance for us of understanding the importance of signs and symbols is that those of us involved in the education of young people are responsible for inducting them into worlds made up of symbols – the things that are our cultural tools. We are thinking here of inducting children into the world of reading and writing and mathematics, as well as art and music. You will know that letters, *ideograms*, musical notes and numerals are all symbols. They all, alone or in combination, stand for something else. Here are some examples:

- The numerals 1, 2, 3 stand for 'one', 'two' and 'three'. The words 'one', 'two' and 'three' stand for 'one object', 'two objects', 'three objects'.
- =, – and + are symbols to represent the mathematical concepts or processes of two or more things being the same or equal, the process of taking one amount away from another, or the process of putting one amount together with another.

You can see from these examples how much more difficult it is to describe the process in words than it is in symbols. The symbols summarise concepts. You can think of it as shorthand for concepts.

Here are some more symbols for you to consider:

What does this represent? ✉

You will almost certainly recognise this as the symbol for email

54 Sandra Smidt

Or this? ☺

You may use this 'emoticon' yourself to show pleasure or approval. It is often used in texting or emailing.

Or this?

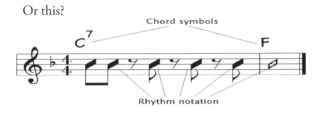

This is musical notation and it is more complex to decode. Each of the marks in it represents something. The first symbol which is the curly thing on the left-hand side of the diagram tells you which part of an instrument the music should be played on. It is the sign to say it should be played in the treble clef (the highest voice). The second (which looks like a small b sitting on a line) tells you which key the music is in and indicates which notes should be played as they are and which need to be shifted either up or down by one half-step. The third (which looks like two 4s on top of one another) tells you how many beats there are in a bar. The black marks on sticks are the notes you play and the hooked shape between them tells you not to play. A complex system but one which tells you exactly what to do when you play an instrument or sing. One of the most important things is that having this kind of written notation means that something is recorded for all time. Every time someone plays a piece of music or reads a poem or a book, the music or the words remain exactly the same. This is not to suggest that there is no space for improvisation but rather that things can be kept as they are and this is particularly important in the case of books or poems or music that are regarded as highly significant for any group.

Vygotsky was insistent that children's consciousness (which you will remember is their awareness) comes from others – adults and children – and it exists only in response to a world which is social. So through their interactions (through their play and exploration in this social world) children acquire signs or symbols which are of use to them and they then use these themselves to interact and explain. Dyson (1997) says that the gap between the child and a more expert other in terms of understanding the signs they have appropriated becomes an *interactive space* where common meanings and signs are negotiated. This is how Vygotsky believed that children grow into the intellectual life of those around them. What he meant by that was that children become part of the thinking of their own group or culture. This is why some children arrive at the nursery, aged only three, with already determined ideas about things like what boys can do, what girls are not able to do, why making guns is wrong, why they should always get their own way and so on.

Looking back, looking ahead

In this chapter we have looked in more detail at what is meant by development and at how that relates to culture. So we have seen that while the word development describes observable events, the word culture allows some *analysis* of understandable events. We have looked, too, at how important culture is to personal identity and to links to others and tried to imagine what a culture feels like to someone new to it. Finally, we started to look at symbols as cultural tools. We return to these themes later in this book.

In the next chapter we start to examine in more detail perhaps the most important cultural tool – language itself. This requires us to think more carefully about signs and symbols and about the social nature of learning.

Glossary

Word or phrase	What it means	Why it is significant
accomplishments	A synonym for achievements.	
analysis	A way of examining something in detail in order to understand more about it.	Something we strive to do when we try and understand what we see or hear or read.
asili nidi	The Italian word for nursery provision for babies and toddlers.	
biology	The science of life and living organisms.	It is important to know that there are many influences on children and the first is biology – what they are born with as well as what affects them throughout life.
culturally constructed	This term means how members of a group create shared meanings and values.	An essential ingredient in learning is to both use and create shared meanings and values.
culture	All the socially passed on beliefs and values, arts and tools, thoughts and institutions that are the products of human work and thinking.	Essential for understanding anything at all about learning and teaching.

development	The process by which an individual or a group or system moves organically and changes in the process.	It is important to know that development and learning are linked but not synonymous.
developmental niches	This term is used to describe the physical and social settings, historically constructed customs and practices of childcare and child rearing and psychology of those involved with children which are shared by a culture.	A useful term to help us understand the different worlds and systems children can inhabit.
elementary or lower processes	Basic processes like reflexes and automatic responses.	We need to know about these terms in order to understand how they become changed, through interaction and the use of tools, to higher processes.
exosystem	The environment beyond home and school and including doctors and shops and so on.	Part of Bronfenbrenner's ecological analysis of society which helps us understand interconnecting systems.
ideograms	A symbolic way of representing something using pictorial rather than alphabetic signs.	Important to know that not all written systems are the same or even similar.
intrinsic	This means essential.	
macrosystem	The widest environmental set of factors which impact on the life of the child: things like national laws.	Part of Bronfenbrenner's ecological analysis of society which helps us understand interconnecting systems.

material tool	A tool which is actual rather than symbolic – such as a pen or a hammer or a guitar, and so on.	The use of tools, both material and cultural or psychological, is essential in learning.
mesosystem	Where the culture of the home and the immediate environment interact.	Part of Bronfenbrenner's ecological analysis of society which helps us understand interconnecting systems.
microsystem	The immediate environment of the child at home and close to it.	Part of Bronfenbrenner's ecological analysis of society which helps us understand interconnecting systems.
routines of the day	The things that are essential for living together. For babies these are sleeping, eating, and being changed and so on.	In working with young children it is important to remember that these are essential sites for interaction and hence learning.
semiotics	The system of signs and symbols.	Essential for us to know about these systems which constitute some of the main cultural tools.
signs	A sign is something that stands for or represents something else.	Essential for us to know about these systems which constitute some of the main cultural tools.
stand for	An everyday term which means make something behave like or appear like something else.	
symbols	Something that stands for or represents something else.	Essential for us to know about these systems which constitute some of the main cultural tools.

Chapter 4

On language, concepts and thinking

In this chapter we move on to think about language, which Vygotsky regarded as the most significant of the 'complex signalisation systems'. In his book *Thought and Language* (first published in 1934 and frequently reprinted thereafter, sometimes with different titles, e.g. *Thinking and Speaking*) Vygotsky explained the explicit and deep connection between speech and thought. He was interested in how both silent inner speech and spoken language related to thinking. In essence he believed that *inner speech* developed from external speech by becoming internalised, with the younger child having first to think out loud before being able to think without the assistance of speech. Perhaps you can see the similarities here with memory, which also becomes internalised as thought. Thought, like speech, is social in origin.

Internalisation

Internalisation is one of the most fundamental concepts in Vygotsky's work. I have mentioned it earlier but it is essential to return to it now since it is a crucial part of understanding how we come to be able to think. The central question is how human beings become able to remember and reflect on objects, people, problems and situations when they are no longer present – i.e. in the absence of physical cues. What happens when something is internalised is that the learner begins to be able to gain control over *external processes*, which means being able to use signs and symbols as a cultural tool. For example, once the learner has gained control of the semiotic system of written language, she can invent a story and write it down, consciously controlling the words and letters she selects and the rules of grammar she uses in order to ensure that it is comprehensible and logical. This, as you will appreciate, involves many higher mental concepts.

But let us go back a bit and see what happens with younger children. The young child performs actions or uses words or cultural tools and signals without fully understanding their significance. Think about the young child who is always told to say 'thank you' when given something and does so without understanding the reasons why. What the child does know is that this action gets a positive response from significant adults in her world but she doesn't really understand why saying one word or phrase is regarded as 'polite' while not saying it is regarded as 'rude'.

In a similar way a child may know the meaning of a word but not understand its broader reference; in other words, a matter of not being able to generalise. We will discuss this in more depth later, but, for now, think about a child who can use the word 'apple' to refer to red apples which are her favourite, without yet knowing that the word can also apply to a green apple, a cooked apple, a crab apple, apple sauce and so on. Nouns are used to to refer to objects and in the early stages of acquiring spoken language children's vocabularies consist primarily of nouns. This is because they are attached to objects and their meaning is immediate and clear. But coming to use them in different contexts or for groups of objects requires the higher mental function of being able to generalise. Two points emerge from this:

1. An adult and child in interaction may agree that they are talking about a particular object – perhaps an apple. The younger child may not yet have grasped the fuller meaning of the word and it will take time for her to know that an apple belongs to the category of fruit. Learning that it is a fruit but not a vegetable will take even longer. The processes involved include coming to understand which features of an object allow it to be included in a category and which feature of an object is the defining one in allowing it to belong to a category.
2. Children may use words or concepts in a childlike rather than an adult way. The child might know that an apple is 'nice' or 'juicy' but the adult concept of 'nutritious' may be too difficult.

Internalisation changes the complexity of what is done and at first this is for the worse. The cultural tools to assist memory, for example, are more sophisticated than the skills they take over from and so the learner, at first, uses these clumsily and with some difficulty. We are interested in how the cultural tool of language is linked to thought and this involves the process of internalisation. Read on.

Piaget and Vygotsky on language and thought

You will almost certainly have heard of Jean Piaget and have very probably come across his ideas. He is best known for his stage theory of development in which he proposed that children all pass through clear age-related stages of development, moving from a first stage where exploration is through senses and movement to a final stage of formal operations.

Piaget's work has been influential in many Western education systems and has contributed much to our understanding of learning and development. But Piaget's theories do not take significant account of a child's social environment, and for him the role of the adult is primarily in the choice of activities and resources. While language, for Piaget, is clearly a symbolic system for representing the world, it is quite separate from the actions which lead to reasoning and the development of logical thinking. One idea that arises from this is that it is of little use to explain things verbally to young children before they are 'ready', i.e. at the right stage in development to understand the ideas behind the explanation. 'Readiness' became something much talked about in educational circles.

Vygotsky had access to the work of Piaget, although the reverse was not true. He read, with interest, Piaget's ideas on speech and thought. Piaget believed that a child's first, emergent use of speech was what he called *autistic*, by which he meant it was related only to the child's own needs and desires. Socialised speech and logic, for him, did not appear until later, with *egocentric* speech and its associated thought being what he called the genetic link between autism and logic. For Vygotsky, however, the child's earliest speech was already social, in the sense that it is always about communication with others. When *he* used the term 'egocentric speech' he was referring to a transition from outer speech to inner speech. In short this means that in the first stages of development children need to verbally express what they are doing or thinking. That is egocentric speech. When the child no longer needs to vocalise thought the egocentric speech has been internalised. So what was outer speech has become inner speech.

Vygotsky was influenced in his thinking about this by the work of Charlotte Buhler, whose research had shown that children under the age of one year already used vocal activity as a way of making social contact. How children acquire their first language is a complex and fascinating study in its own right and we will only touch on it in this book. Basically, the human infant learns the meanings of signs or symbols through interactions with others – primarily the mother or other caregivers. The infant also hears the sounds of the language or languages of the home and makes attempts to replicate these.

Through the vignettes that follow you get an emerging picture of children imitating the sounds they hear, developing the muscles needed for the production of sound, engaging in making and sharing meaning using this and other means like pointing, and finally beginning to name and categorise. They are examples of early vocalising and language play, moving from imitation and practice to real communication. They are all drawn from the developmental diaries kept by the children's mothers and given to the author.

> Eta chatters to herself, usually in her cot, making sounds like 'aba aba' or 'da' and 'ba'.

> Thando lies under the tree clicking. She uses her tongue and her lips. Our language (Xhosa) has click sounds in it.

Eta and Thando are both practising the sounds they have heard and their muscle skills in producing them. Did you know that, at birth, babies are potentially able to make the sounds of all human languages but that this ability falls away as they hear and reproduce the sounds of their own language or languages?

> Theo stares at something he wants and sometimes makes noises to accompany this. If we don't understand or respond he stares at us and then at the object he wants. It is very funny!

Theo has learned that pointing can be a tool to accomplish something. Here we see him using eye-pointing where he looks intently at what he wants. He is clearly communicating a need or a desire.

> Demi looked at an orange and I responded by asking 'Do you want this orange? Is this what you want?' as I held up the orange. I was rewarded with a big grin and a nod of the head.

Demi, too, used eye-pointing, and also body language by nodding her agreement to being given an orange. So the communication is a two-way process.

Later the child may start to accompany her actions with sounds – again as a way of communicating her needs or desires. She hears the sounds of her language through all her interactions with family members and learns that sounds can operate as signs which can be used to interact with others and to satisfy needs and desires. It is now that the child starts wanting things named. This is what Nella's mum noted about this:

> We took the children to the zoo and I kept pointing to the animals and saying their names. Nella, who is fifteen months old, kept saying 'cat' and pointing to each animal in turn. It seemed to us that she knew they were animals and her cat is an animal and so she called all the animals 'cat'. Three months later Nella has started going 'Wot dat?' and pointing to the object she wants named. It is constant and exhausting.

Pre-intellectual speech and pre-verbal thought

While analysing the links between spoken language and thought, Vygotsky drew a distinction between what he called pre-intellectual speech and pre-verbal thought. Let us try and define each of these terms:

- *Pre-intellectual speech* is the sort of vocal activity we hear very young children engage in when they use it either for social contact or to practise the sounds of their home languages which they hear throughout their daily lives. Eta and Thando are using what we might call pre-intellectual speech.
- *Pre-verbal thought* is more difficult to understand but Vygotsky used the term to mean what happens when other people direct the child's attention towards or away from something by means of spoken language. So the means is still external to the child. Here is a wonderful example adapted from the work of Daniel Elkonin (1995):

He wrote about his small grandchild Andrei when he was about one year old. Grandfather and child played a game where the child lay down and the grandfather tapped on his foot while reciting a rhyme. At the end of the ritual the grandfather tickled him gently. When the game was over Andrei would take his grandfather's hand, direct it to his foot and invite him to continue the game. This makes me think of the example of Hannah signalling that she wanted to continue a game of having her feet lifted and dropped by stretching her leg and pointing her toes.

For Vygotsky pre-intellectual speech was what he described as 'primitive' and took place without intellectual activity, or thinking. This is not to suggest that young children don't think but rather that their thinking can take place without the support of speech and language. There can be vocal activity without thought, and thought without vocal activity.

Vygotsky charted the development of the speech–thought relationship in stages or phases as follows:

1. An initial phase where the motor and speech aspects of the child's behaviour are fused. Speech in this phase is *referential* (related to something the child can see or wants), *object-orientated* (related to a thing or object) and *social* (in order to communicate). Each of the examples below illustrates one or more of these.

In the first example the speech is object-oriented: the child is naming or referring to the 'object' (i.e. the baby). The child does not want or need the baby but is commenting on something in her world, practising, perhaps, her skill at naming:

> The mother, carrying her child down the road, hears the child say 'baby' which directs her attention to a baby in the pram in front of them.

In the next example the speech is referential. The child, seeing a banana in a shop window, indicates that she wants one to eat:

> 'Nana' said Umut, pointing to the window of the fruit shop.

The final example is in order to communicate. It is both telling the others in the room something and a shout of pleasure and greeting:

> 'Daddy!' shouts Uli, as he sees his father's car coming up the road.

Because the child is surrounded by more expert speakers and thinkers, over time the child's speech begins to take on more and more demonstrative features which allow the child to show his needs and feelings.

The child told to put his toys away stamps his foot and shouts, 'Won't! Mummy do it!'

2   The child then begins to be able to use *correct forms of grammar* and has a *growing vocabulary* but the language may not be directly related to what the child is doing.

3   The next phase is where the child uses spoken language to explain or describe things for herself or for others. This speech is called *inner speech* or *monologue* and is an important precursor to conscious thought.

This is an example taken from the work of Rosa Levina, one of the members of Vygotsky's group. She tells us of a four-year-old child who was trying to get some candy which had been placed too high for her to reach. The child talked herself through the problem as she solved it. This monologue or inner speech clearly accompanied her actions. In this way speech and problem-solving came together in the child's running commentary. She climbed onto the divan and jumped up as she tried to reach the candy and as she did so she said aloud, to herself, something like 'That candy is up too high… I will have to call Mommy so she will get it for me. There's no way I can reach it, it's so high.' The child then picked up a stick and looked at the candy, saying, 'Papa has a big cupboard and sometimes he can reach things.' She managed to use the stick to knock the sweets off the shelf and then decided that the stick was so useful to her in solving her problem that she would take it home with her.

4   It is only when this inner speech becomes *internalised* (which means it may no longer be spoken or evident to anyone other than the child) that the child uses it *privately, internally* and *consciously to solve problems*. Think carefully about each of those words because they are important. We have explained the meaning of 'privately' and 'internally' but the significance of 'consciously' is that it has become a tool of thinking available to the child in the sense that she can choose to use it. You will remember reading about internalisation in a previous chapter.

To remind you, here is an example drawn from the work of Kenner (2004). She describes how Yazan experimented with the directionality of print in English and Arabic. Asked by one of his peers to write his name in English, he attempted to write it using Arabic directionality, going from right to left instead of left to right. Kenner suggests that he seemed to be asking himself (using internalised speech), 'What happens if you write English from right to left?' On another occasion he wrote his sister's name in English script with the first name going from right to left and the second name from left to right (Kenner 2004: 97). He was solving a problem he had set himself without using speech.

In summary then, Vygotsky felt that the development of the speech–thought continuum went through four stages or phases:

1. A *primitive* stage, where speech and vocalisation are used to make contact and express emotions and where the child can engage in systematic and goal-directed activity without resorting to speech. This is the phase of pre-intellectual speech. Here speech and thought are separate.
2. A stage of *practical intelligence*, where the child's language uses *syntactic* and *logical* forms (perhaps using grammatical forms such as sentences, questions and statements) which have parallels in what the child is doing but may not be linked to it.
3. A third stage where the child starts to use *external symbolic* means, like language or other cultural tools, to help with internal problem-solving. We observe this when we see/hear children engage in inner speech.
4. In the fourth stage the child *internalises the symbolic tools* and engages in problem-solving thought without vocalising it overtly. Language that accompanies problem-solving activities often demonstrates the learner using language to reflect on what is happening rather than as a prop to aid thinking.

As we have already noted, Piaget regarded *egocentric speech* as speech that did not require a listener or an audience. He saw it as speech carried out by a young child with pleasure and satisfaction, even in the absence of any listener. You will have heard young children doing this – often when they are alone in their cots at night or in their prams in the garden or lying on a rug under a tree. They engage in monologues, repetitions, comments on life and experiences. While for Piaget there was no social basis for this, for Vygotsky there was. Nonetheless he accepted Piaget's definition and felt that this egocentric speech offered a window on the processes operating during the silent, what one might call 'speech-for-oneself' phase on the road to the verbal thinking which is so evident in older children and adults. So as we have said, egocentric speech is a passing or transitory phenomenon.

Vygotsky designed a series of experiments in which the aspects and features and purposes of inner speech and internalised speech could be addressed.

- In one experiment he offered an activity for the children in which they became very engaged – perhaps drawing or playing. At some point during the activity something interfered with what the children were doing and the children encountered some obstacle or a problem to be solved. He then measured the output of egocentric speech and concluded that when the children were faced with a problem to be solved they began to vocalise their thoughts. *Inner speech was used to help them solve a problem.*
- In another series of experiments he was concerned to show that egocentric speech remained connected to the sphere of social communication from

which it originated. In other words, children using egocentric speech operate on the assumption that what they say will be understood by others, even though the purpose of the speech is not directly social. In order to test this he first measured the levels of egocentric speech during an activity and then introduced something into the situation which meant that the child would encounter someone who could not understand what she was saying. He sometimes introduced a child with a hearing loss into the room, or a child not speaking the same language as the child in the experiment, or put the child very far away from other children in the room or introduced very loud external noise. What happened was that the number of utterances diminished in all these cases showing clearly that *children, speaking out loud, did so in the expectation of being understood.*

After Vygotsky's death research into egocentric speech continued with researchers paying attention to the speech-in-private of infants and young children. This speech, sometimes called *acommunicative speech* (which means speech not for communication) appears to be more complex than had been thought and ranges from simple repetition to complex and elaborate dialogues with an imaginary partner. Some of the research suggests that this speech plays an important role in language practice as children, through imitation, memory, repetition and modification, rehearse and improve their own grammatical constructions and compare old and new utterances:

> Sammy, in her bed in the early morning: 'Sitting, oppositting, sitting, oppositting.' She seemed to be trying out the validity of a word she had invented to describe the concept of 'sitting opposite' someone.

Understanding concepts

Embedded in Vygotsky's thinking is the theory that the *concepts* (or understandings) children form are not fixed but evolve or develop over time. He argued that we may not be able to talk about child logic but we can track how thinking, logic and problem-solving change over time, through experience and interactions. In order to demonstrate this he used a methodological approach developed by his colleague Lev Sacharov. This involved using a set of 22 blocks which varied in colour, shape, height and size. On the underside of each block was written a nonsense word. These were *lag, bik, mur* and *sev*. You will notice that each is made up of three letters. The word *lag*, however, was always written on the underside of all the large tall blocks; *bik* on all flat large figures; *mur* on the tall small ones and *sev* on the flat small ones. The blocks were placed randomly in the centre of a specially made board on which were four corner areas. The experimenter picked up a sample block, showed it to the subject and read its 'name' after which the subject was invited to select other blocks that might belong to the same kind and put them all in one of the corner areas. When the sorting task was complete the experimenter picked up one of the incorrectly selected blocks, read its name and invited the subject to try again.

According to Vygotsky there were two interacting sets of features presented to the subject: the physical properties of the blocks, and the names of the blocks. The aim was to see when the verbal (the names) and the non-verbal (the properties) became a fully functional cognitive system. The design of the test allowed the process to be repeated over and over again, allowing the subject to move from using one set of properties or more to solve the problem.

His conclusion was that concept formation was only fixed and mature at adolescence, with younger children using what he called *functional equivalence* of concepts. What he meant by this was that, for the youngest children, the problem was solved according to some feeling they had about the blocks and their properties. So they might make such comments as: 'I like these ones', or 'These go together'. More advanced thinkers moved through using properties of the blocks themselves and grouping them according to these potential concepts – perhaps sorting them by colour or by size or by shape, and finally to pseudoconcepts. This is the stage, for Vygotsky, where the thinker is capable of what he called *logical thought*.

A reminder, at this point, that Vygotsky believed that the social activity of speaking was directly connected with the active process of thinking. Thinking, as we have seen, was, for him, a culturally mediated social process of communication.

From everyday concepts to scientific concepts

As we begin to chart the move from everyday concepts to scientific concepts we begin to encounter Vygotsky's thoughts on teaching and pedagogy. Let us start as we so often do by defining these ideas:

- *Everyday concepts*, as you might imagine, are the concepts children encounter through their interactions and activity in the everyday worlds of home and community. You will remember that the process by which children acquire concepts is mediated by the cultural tool of speech. So as children play and interact with others they develop concepts, which are called either everyday concepts or *spontaneous concepts*. These might relate to cooking, or eating, or going to the clinic, or sickness, or birth of a baby brother, or starting school, or going on holiday, and so on. In other words, through their interaction, and mediated by speech, children learn the concepts relating to their lives. For Vygotsky and for others the strength of these everyday concepts is that they have arisen from direct, usually *first-hand experience* and have not relied on memory. Those of us involved in the care and education of young children know about this, even though we may never have used the terms 'everyday concepts' or 'spontaneous concepts'. We know about the importance of the experiences children have had before school or setting and during school and setting, but within the children's everyday lives of home and community.

- *Scientific concepts* are those that arise through some type of instruction more often in a formal system of knowledge rather than through interactions in everyday life. The child, in a formal educational setting, is exposed to some of the abstract conceptual knowledge of her culture. A child in a school in Kenya, for example, may be learning about some abstract concepts in common with a child in Sussex (dark and light, perhaps or long and short), but also some very different concepts (uses of cow dung as fuel, for example). Through interactions with a more knowledgeable person, adult or child, the learner is introduced to these more abstract and general concepts.

In a fascinating article on children learning everyday concepts, Jane and Robbins (2007) illustrate how their grandchildren acquire concepts relating to science and technology. Most children will first learn about these things in formal settings. But in their small piece of research the children acquired them through their rich interactions with grandparents. In the research the grandparents themselves notice how what starts off as children acquiring everyday concepts through discussions and activities alongside the adults changes when the children begin to internalise and then reflect on their developing understandings.

> Oliver at the beach wanted to know why there were bits of glass that were really smooth and asked, 'Granddad, where does the sea go when the tide goes out?' (Jane and Robbins 2004: 4)

> Ben, aged 7, strung a complex set of strands across the living room and then found ways of putting his bionicles and a set of small figures onto them in order for them to slide down. He invented pulleys and hammocks and when one of the figures fell to the floor immediately set up a 'hospital' in a corner of the kitchen, fashioned a plaster cast of onion skin and a crutch out of toothpicks and comforted the wounded figure, reflecting out loud 'That must have been very painful!' (Personal observation: see Figure 4.1)

Here, in the context of real-life experience, we see children exploring complex everyday concepts through their interactions and speech. Speech is the cultural tool with which learning is mediated. It is at first *intermental* – which means it occurs through interaction *between* people engaged in a joint sociocultural activity – and later becomes *intramental* – which means that it takes place *within* the child. It takes place inside the child through the process of internalisation.

Gordon Wells (1994) studied both everyday and scientific concepts and arrived at a set of four features which, for him, define scientific concepts. He called these generality, systematic organisation, conscious awareness and voluntary control. The examples which illustrate them come from seven-year-old Manjeet, talking about his class topic on magnets.

68 Sandra Smidt

Figure 4.1 Ben's figure, with onion-skin plaster cast and toothpick crutch

1 *Generality* implies the quality of including particulars.

   The teacher asked us to think about magnets in class to try and think what things would be attracted by them. I thought it would include all metals.

2 *Systematic organisation* refers to the ways in which abstract concepts are hierarchically ordered in some cases and which allow for ideas relating to them to be tested out in some way.

   To find out if our first ideas were correct we had to find things we thought would stick to the magnets and try them out. I wasn't always right.

3 *Conscious awareness* means that the child is able to articulate her own understanding of the concept.

   I know that magnets attract metal objects and I learned that magnets have poles but I am not sure I really understand what they are or what they do. I keep thinking of polar bears and things like that. My teacher laughed when I told her that.

4 *Voluntary control* means that the child can almost choose what to know.

   I really loved that topic about magnets because it was great fun to use so many different things to see which were attracted and which were – what's that word again? Oh, yeah. Repelled.

For Vygotsky scientific concepts begin with abstract verbal definitions. Here are some to consider:

- Magnets attract metal objects.
- Even numbers are divisible by two.
- A past participle indicates something that happened previously.

There is much more you can read about concept development and about Vygotsky's thoughts on words and meaning but that is beyond the scope of this book.

The importance of reflection

Vygotsky believed that all speech was social in its origins and functions. This does not mean that all speech requires an audience. He also saw that there could be speech without thought and thought without speech. We often find this hard to understand but it is clear that some people think through images and some through mathematical functions and some through other means. The early vocalisations of children which accompany their actions and their attempts to solve problems are known as inner speech and it is only when this becomes internalised that conscious thought is achieved. *Conscious thought implies the ability to think about or reflect on what has been learned. This is extremely significant in terms of learning.* For example, children who have access to more than one language from birth begin to be able to reflect on the similarities and differences between two symbolic systems and in doing this become aware of what they know about language itself. They are developing metacognitive skills. *Metacognition* can be defined as knowledge about knowledge itself. It is not clear whether or not Vygotsky used the term metacognitive but his explanation of internalisation indicates that a learner becoming conscious of what she knows and has learned has reached a higher mental function. Certainly, since Vygotsky's death researchers have paid attention to the importance of reflection in learning, and the recent research of Kenner (2004a, b) and Gregory *et al.* (2004), for example, shows how powerful a tool it is as children teach one another and as they do it reflect on what they already know and can do.

Looking ahead, looking back

In this chapter we have looked at the distinctions Vygotsky made between social speech and inner speech and at how he believed speech becomes internalised in order to allow for thought and reflection. We have looked, too, at his ideas about how children form concepts and this takes us, for the first time, to the fringes of exploring his ideas about teaching and learning. You have encountered some difficult concepts in this chapter but once these have been internalised you (like the children with whom you work and interact) will be able to reflect on what you have learned.

In the coming chapter we start to look at the implications for our practice of what we have studied so far. We shall revisit the main themes addressed so far – mediation, culture, cultural tools, concepts, language and so on – and use these as the foundation for a Vygotskian perspective on pedagogy or teaching.

Glossary

Word or phrase	What it means	Why it is significant
acommunicative speech	Speech which is used without having communication as its aim.	Another Piagetian concept.
autistic	Related to the child's immediate needs.	
complex signalisation systems	Systems for communication, of which language is the most important.	
concepts	Thoughts or ideas: and in Vygotsky's thinking he talked of elementary or everyday concepts, which arise through experience of meaningful situations, often handling objects, and scientific concepts, which arise through teaching.	Extremely important in Vygotsky's thinking and hence for us to consider.
conscious awareness	The ability to know what it is you have achieved or know.	Higher order function.
consciously	When the learner is aware of something.	A higher order concept.
egocentric speech	Defined differently by Piaget and Vygotsky: the latter saw it as the transition between inner and outer speech.	Very important to know about all aspects of speech, the audible signs of thinking in the early stages.

intermental	This means between people – so people sharing ideas.	Children move from coming to understand something through interactions …
intramental	This means within an individual – to so private thinking.	… to being able to do this on their own. Do you see the link to the ZPD?
logical thought	The ability to make one thing link to another in order to make sense of something.	A higher order function.
monologue	The speech used by children as they do something. It later becomes internalised.	Essential to understand the role of monologue in thinking.
object-oriented speech	The speech of very young children used to refer to things that are usually evident and sometimes present.	Useful to linguists or others studying the development of language.
pre-intellectual speech	Speech without thought.	This is something that is perfectly possible, according to Vygotsky.
pre-verbal thinking	Thinking without speech.	This is also possible and might involve the use of other cultural tools – music or mathematical symbols or drawing, for example.
referential speech	A linguistic term used to refer to one- or two-word utterances used by young children to refer to something.	Useful to linguists or others studying the development of language.
scientific concepts	These are the concepts acquired through direct teaching and are often related to abstract thoughts.	A higher order function.
syntax	The grammar of something or the rules which hold it together.	

| systematic organisation | A way of things being structured in a logical fashion. | |
| voluntary control | The ability to make decisions about what to do. | Higher order function. |

Chapter 5

Learning and teaching

We are now going to look back at the first four chapters and consider what they tell us about teaching and learning. In doing this we will analyse the ideas we have come across in order to learn more about how we can support the learning and development of the children in our care. Throughout the chapter this symbol will indicate a section with particular relevance to your teaching.

Taking a sociohistorical stance

In the first chapter you read about Vygotsky's life and about the influences on him. In other words, we started by considering the influence of where and when he was born, the context of his family and community, the people he encountered within his family and further afield, the effect of his education at home, at high school and at university, and the influence of what he read and heard through his many discussions and encounters. The approach is social because it looks at what interactions he had and with whom; it is historical because it sets his own life history in the context of a broader history. This sociohistorical account allows us to understand him and his ideas within the context of time and place. Those of us working with young children are very aware of the importance of knowing as much as possible about the children with whom we work. We understand that children learn through their interactions and through all their experiences and so this sort of approach is familiar to us. In many schools and and other settings information about the child's life prior to entering the school or setting is gathered on entry. However, this is often carried out in a manner that is not appropriately adapted to the very real needs of many parents who may not be familiar with the system their child is entering; they may have English as an additional language; they may be working so hard that time itself is precious. Many schools and settings ask parents to complete a form, sometimes on the premises with help but often at home. Information collected is often used for purely statistical purposes and may not even be seen by the teaching staff.

You may want to read through the following example of a system developed by a particular children's centre and see if it offers you ideas which may influence your own practice:

At the Madiba Children's Centre much care and attention is paid to how children and their families are introduced to the centre. This is based on the awareness by the staff of the importance of establishing good links with families and communities in order to know more about the child's early life and in order to build a partnership to benefit the child and the family. To start with, when parents visit the centre they are taken round by someone who speaks their home language (where possible) and they are invited to watch what the children do, and how they interact with one another and with the adults. They are also invited to ask any questions. Following that a home visit is arranged, providing that the parents or carers are happy for this to take place. Someone from the centre visits the family at home, spends some time with the child and brings with them a book containing photographs of different activities, information about the centre (available in the main languages of the community) and a form which asks for both statistical and additional information. Details such as date of birth, inoculations and position in family are collected, together with information about languages spoken at home, the child's early experience, relationships with key people (parents, siblings, grandparents, other family members, people in the community and so on), and likes, dislikes, fears and passions. This form is completed by the parents or carer together with the worker from the centre. In this way a face-to-face dialogue is set up, the start of a partnership at the beginning of the child's life away from home.

Carlina Rinaldi (2006), who has spent her life working for the wonderful early years provision in Reggio Emilia, has considered carefully some of the issues facing both parents and educators when the child moves from home to setting or school. Importantly she warns against judgements made by parents about educators or educators about parents. In her view there is no such thing as either a good or a bad parent. We have to avoid stereotypes and superficial judgements which risk undermining the possibility of building respectful relationships with those whose experiences are different from ours. She notes, too, the changes in the lives of young families in today's world, with the collapse of the extended family and the need for parents to either study or work, or both, in order to fulfil their lives and feed their families. She suggests that we need to think carefully how we communicate with all parents in terms of formal and informal communication. We may need to move the focus to thinking about the child as an already *competent learner*, paying attention to what the child is already doing and learning and achieving. The process of education and care becomes a two-way process, in which the child learns more about the world and the educator learns more about the child and the child's world. She talks, too, of using new tools to show the child's journey – photographs and videos and slides and images, which reveal the amazing things the child says and does in her time at the school or setting. Finally, she talks of new methods to build ways of meeting together to share information and feelings, at times and in places that address the life needs of parents and carers.

What do we learn from this?

In terms of sensitive and effective teaching and learning we must start by finding out as much as we can about the life of the child. We want to know what the child has shown interest in and been involved in, at home and in the local community. We want to know who the important people in the child's life are. We want to know what the child likes, what she fears, what she enjoys, and what significant experiences she has had. This is a double-edged tool. In the first place it allows us to begin to build on the child's prior experience; in the second it marks the beginning of a two-way partnership with parents and carers. Understanding the child's experiences, culture and cultural tools, networks of support and communication, and significant others (adult and peer) allows us to begin to build another world for the child to learn in and from, and to offer another culture to which the child contributes. This is the culture of the classroom or setting – another sociohistorical marker on each child's journey through life. As Luria said:

> We should not look for the explanation of behaviour in the depths of the brain or the soul but in the external living conditions of persons and most of all in the external conditions of their societal life, in their social-historical forms of existence.
>
> (1979: 23)

Mediation and cultural tools

In Chapter 2 we started to consider what is an ongoing theme in Vygotsky's work, namely mediation. He was insistent that our interactions with the world are always mediated through the use of the signs or cultural tools of our society. The signs are social (made by people in groups in response to needs and values) and include such things as language; counting systems, mnemonic techniques and algebraic symbols; paintings and sculptures; music; writing; and diagrams and plans and mechanical drawings as well as road signs. For the children in our care each interaction with the physical or the social world is mediated through the signs or cultural tools available. Just to confuse the issue Wertsch (1981) tells us that it is possible to find two meanings of mediation in Vygotsky's work. These relate to Vygotsky's life and the particular language he used with different groups of people at different times in his life. Early in his life, when he was exploring psychology itself, he talked of mediation in the sense of it being particular to an individual learner. Perhaps the child is exploring something through language, or alongside someone else. In each of these examples the mediation is *explicit*. Later in his life Vygotsky became more involved in the world of pedagogy and he began to think of mediation as perhaps being sometimes *less explicit* or *implicit*. This was when he referred to the role of inner speech – speech that is not visible or audible or evident. This is a cultural tool which mediates learning, just as more explicit forms do, such as getting particular help from a more expert other. Moving from a dependence on explicit forms to being able to access less explicit forms of mediation the child becomes an independent thinker. What is important about this type of implicit mediation is that it is not something constructed by the educator, but embedded in the class context, the ongoing communicative stream that accompanies action. Let us try and step back from this, think about it and try to see what messages it has for us as educators.

For me this aspect of Vygotsky's work is important in terms of the social and cultural notions it carries with it. When he states that all learning is social, he means that children will learn through their interactions with others – both adults and peers – and that it involves cultural tools which are the signs and semiotic systems developed within cultures and passed on and transformed by those within the culture. Annabel, at the age of one, was playing, on her own, with some rods and balls with holes into which the rods could be fitted. Her grandmother was intrigued to see her first putting her finger into the hole before trying a rod. What was she doing? Was she asking herself the question, 'If my finger goes in and the rod goes in are they the same in some way?' Of course she doesn't yet have the language – the cultural tool – for asking this question, but something complex is going on in that little brain. And how can we say this is an example of learning being social? Consider the fact that the toys she is playing with have been made and are, for her, cultural tools. Consider too that she lives in a family in which she has an older sibling, parents and grandparents. Consider that she hears spoken language and songs and rhymes and stories. All of this is social and all of it contributes to everything she learns.

What do we learn from this?

Take a look at your classroom or setting and see what cultural tools you can identify and then ask yourself what it feels like to be a child – any one of the individual children in your group. To help you here are some vignettes to consider.

> Umut has moved from London to a small town in Sussex. He had only been in his setting for two months when the family was moved. He is a Turkish speaker and was just about settling in to his nursery class. At the new class he is the only Turkish speaker, in fact, the only child with English as an additional language. At his old nursery he could hear the sounds of Turkish early in the morning when his dad brought him to his class and one of the nursery nurses was a Turkish speaker. There were some books and stories on CD in English and Turkish and he loved going into the home corner to listen to tapes of Turkish music. Now he is adrift. The teacher says he 'knows nothing' and 'can't listen' and 'won't join in'.
>
> Safia, a Teaching Assistant, is a Turkish speaker who came to London as a small child. She has kept a memory of what it felt like to start school having

English as an additional language, and this memory of losing a culture and being inducted into another has given her a particular sensitivity to the needs of individual children. She has no Turkish speakers in her group this year but there are three little girls who have come from Poland. Although she knew nothing about Poland she has made it her business to make contact with the families and the community to learn as much as possible. Some things were easy to incorporate. The alphabetic system is very similar to the English alphabet. One of the mothers took her to the local Polish shop and they bought some Polish goods – bread and sausage and jams – and one of the activities on offer in the early days when the Polish girls started school was a 'cooking' activity – making sandwiches using the familiar ingredients. The activity seemed to Safia to be universal. After all, in all cultures food plays a vital role. And the choosing of fillings, the buttering of the bread, the cutting of the slices are all activities full of meaning and wonderful opportunities for using two sets of cultural tools – spoken English and spoken Turkish.

Malane and her family come from South Africa. As a baby Malane was carried on her mother's back, tied in a blanket. This was customary in her village and provided her with the opportunity, from soon after birth, of being a silent participant (at first) in all aspects of life in the village. She would hear her mother talking and the sounds of her first language, IsiZulu; she would hear the sound of the grain being ground, of the women singing, of the children chanting, of the cows lowing. Coming to live in Glasgow was difficult for her family and they were delighted to find that at the Children's Centre they had lots of singing, and opportunities to play with dolls of all colours and to carry them on your back or in a papoose or in a pram. And her new key worker wanted to learn as much as possible about her early life in South Africa. Her parents have been so pleased that Malane has found some familiar things in this new world, and that enable her to part from them each day with ease.

When Joshua and his family went to live in France and he started school, his family were upset that the children – aged only 7 and 8 – were asked not to talk in class. His parents wrote in a letter to their relatives that going into a silent room full of little children with their heads down gave them a deep sense of unease. They had both believed that learning – particularly for younger children, but all the way through school and even university – meant exchanging ideas, comparing thoughts, commenting, questioning and celebrating.

One aim of any teaching is to enable students themselves to become fluent users of the culture's sign systems. You have only to think of how much time you devote to ensuring that children in early years settings learn to chant the alphabet, write their names, perhaps read simple statements, count objects, name objects, sort objects, compare objects. All of this – the mastering of semiotic tools

– begins with interaction, on the social plane. So a child first encountering a new cultural tool usually does so through the interactions and participation of more experienced users. The child participates in this social interaction and it is here that the child starts to try to interpret what is happening. Now this interpretation and explanation can take place at different levels, and you will know from your own experience just how little understanding one needs to have to operate in the modern world. How many of us know what physically happens when we send an email? But the use of the cultural tool of language may well mean that we are forced to say more (and maybe also less) than we actually understand or intend. Wertsch (1981) argues (and you may not agree with him) that this saying of things we don't yet understand fully is desirable because it seems to force us to go further to try to ensure understanding. Indeed, for me, in writing this book, grappling with concepts like mediation has often forced me to use inner speech – thinking aloud – in order to clarify and internalise what I am discovering.

Memory and thought

Learning is a journey which begins with trying to make sense of the world and the objects and people in it. During this exploration others are encountered and these others are usually more expert so they offer models and language or other cultural tools to assist the learner. Over time the learner is able to remember and use what has been internalised. In Vygotskian speech this is the journey from natural or individual forms of behaviour to higher mental functions. This is a very crude explanation of Vygotsky's laws which he called the general *genetic laws*. Summarised, the laws that Vygotsky initially formulated state that:

1   The law of *transition* or the law of mediation, which tracks the move from natural forms of behaviour to cultural forms of behaviour, that are mediated by tools and signs:

    Uri looks at his mother and sees her looking out of the window. He sees the car out of the window and points to it. 'Yes,' says his mother, interpreting the question he cannot yet ask through following the child's gaze. 'Your daddy's home.'

    (Smidt 2006: 38)

In this example the child is paying attention to his mother and to what she does. He notices her looking out of the window, works out that she is looking at something, and uses pointing to get information. It is the behaviour of the more expert other which determines the child's behaviour. This is an example of *intersubjectivity*, the ability to understand the feelings and intentions of others. It will not be long until Uri can hear the car and without prompting reverse the roles by telling his mother that daddy is home. Mediation comes about through the use of signs and language.

2   The law of *sociogenesis*, which charts the transition from the social (sometimes called intermental) to the individual (sometimes called intramental) forms of behaviour.

Nandi is playing with her little sister and as part of the play she is singing her a nursery rhyme – 'Ride a cock horse to Banbury Cross'. The play involves bouncing Kari on her knee. Two days later their mother comes into the room to find Kari bouncing her doll on her knee as she sings her own version of the nursery rhyme.

From the social experience with her sister Kari has internalised the rules of the game and 'sings' along to the required actions. This is a very clear illustration of the social becoming individual.

3   The law of *ingrowth*, which describes the transition of mental functions (or thinking) from without to within. This is where inner speech, for example, becomes internalised.

Abdullah sees his plastic duck on a table which is a little too high for him to reach easily. He goes over to his blue chair and drags it across the room, saying, 'I need this. I can stand on it and then I can get my duck.' A few days later, without saying anything, he climbs onto his blue chair and from there onto the table and looks out of the window.

He had worked out a plan and carried it out, verbalising what he was doing. A few days later he worked out another plan, but clearly related to the first one, and this time did not need to verbalise it. The thinking had become internalised.

You may encounter various accounts of these genetic laws and these vary because both his thinking and the interpretations by translators changed over time. But in essence what the laws describe is the move from dependence on others to independence; the move from needing concrete or direct experience to assist memory to being able to call up memory consciously. If you are familiar with the work of Margaret Donaldson (and some of you will be, e.g. *Children's Minds*, 1978) this may well remind you of her assertion that for young children the *concrete* (which means dealing with real things in *meaningful contexts* where the child can make sense of what the problem is because it makes human sense to her) must come before the *abstract*. Children need first-hand experiences before being able to deal with abstract issues and concepts.

What do we learn from this?

We hope you will be reassured to find that something you may well already do is grounded in theory. Vygotsky's work certainly suggests that those working with young children need to ensure that children are allowed and enabled to learn from their early encounters with objects, problems, situations and tasks. This is most likely if:

- such encounters are rooted in activities whose purpose is clear to the children;
- children have access to using movement and their senses or any other means to help them make sense of what they are exploring;
- children are involved in social interactions with others, either peers or adults, who can offer models, give help or take part;
- children have access to cultural tools, including language.

Classes and settings should offer a range of meaningful activities which allow children to understand the purpose of an activity through building on their previous experience. Planting and growing things; cooking and baking; playing with home-like objects and areas; bathing dolls or babies; setting up a clinic or a garage or a supermarket; having a go at making marks on paper for different purposes; setting the tables for lunch: activities such as these and a host of others offer children contexts in which they are likely to learn. Ensuring that children are not expected to be silent or to work alone or to do meaningless tasks like completing worksheets will further enable learning. And so will ensuring that children are talked to and listened to, that their questioning is encouraged, that their theories are taken seriously and that they can have experience of cultural tools in addition to those embedded in the meaningful contexts. We do, of course, have to interact with children on an individual basis, enabling them to move towards acquiring scientific concepts. Here are some case studies for you to consider. In each one ask yourself if you feel the practice described is likely to enable children to move from using everyday concepts to using everyday and abstract concepts.

The first comes from a chapter in Gregory (2004) by Mary Eunice Romero, called 'Cultural literacy in Pueblo children'. Romero spent time researching the development of concepts relating to literacy as she observed children in Pueblo communities in New Mexico. The people there live in agrarian communal villages and modern homes. There are nineteen languages, in three distinct language groups, and as in much of the world there is a growing tendency for English to be the dominant language. Romero was interested in the socialisation of children and, as she had expected, noticed that they were inducted into all aspects of their own cultures through their interactions, allowing them to become competent members of their group. She observed the children, involved in everyday events alongside the rest of the community, silently absorbing social knowledge, internalising it and, through their interactions, coming to know who they are within this social world. She notes that, from birth, Pueblo children are surrounded by important and influential other adults with whom they interact. This forms an elaborate social web involving parents, siblings, aunts, cousins, grandparents, godparents and other family members. Grandparents are venerated because of their age, which represents the score of cultural knowledge they possess to pass on, and are regarded as essential socialisers of the children. Older siblings also play an important socialisation role since they are often involved in taking responsibility for younger siblings. Then there are traditional leaders who take responsibility for whole groups but who are also involved in socialising the children. All of this takes place within smaller groups or clans, known as moieties. Each group has a moiety house and children are taken there to participate in and observe cultural rituals and knowledge.

Bread is made in large outdoor earth ovens on wood fires. Children are intimately involved in the bread-making routines, at first as infants, watching so that they can be kept safe – but also watching the bread being made. As the child gets older he or she is able to handle objects and is given a small lump of dough to play with. But as the child plays an adult will comment on what the child is doing and when the child, by chance, perhaps, appears to roll the dough the praise given will encourage the child to try again. So through actions the child does something similar to what he or she has seen done and is then praised in doing this. At the age of about two or three the child is given a larger piece of dough and placed next to someone who deliberately models the action of turning it into bread for the child. Again the child's efforts are praised lavishly and when children are about four or five years old they are expected to participate without too much coaxing; but yet again their efforts are overtly valued. Children are clearly learning about how to make the bread eaten in their community, but they are learning less obvious things as well. Romero argues that they are learning cooperation and contribution. Throughout much of this children are silent learners – something Lave and Wenger (1991) call 'legitimate peripheral participation'.

Here you will recognise that the children are involved in everyday concepts – making bread, using cultural tools for doing this; bathed in the cultural tool of language and through observation, social interaction and then direct physical involvement. As they do this they also become able to handle abstract and higher order functions as they internalise what it means to be a member of a group and to work collaboratively. You may want to spend some time observing a morning in your class or setting and checking off what opportunities there are for children to:

- observe someone modelling something and listen to the accompanying verbal exchanges;
- participate in a group activity, perhaps silently at first;
- be praised and supported in their attempts.

The next example also comes from Gregory's book, this time from a chapter written by Manjula Datta and called 'Friendship literacy'. This time we are in an inner city multicultural school in London where three seven-year-old boys are sharing favourite books with one another. The boys are Mehmet, Sam and Daniel: Mehmet is of Turkish origin, Sam of Algerian-French origin and Daniel is a native English speaker. They are sharing a book called *Celebrations* (1997) and the excerpt we are going to examine is where they talk about rituals associated with death – something which concerns many children.

Mehmet: Well, (when) grandpa died ... Do you know in mosques ... when someone dies or when praying there's two places, one for ladies' prayer room upstairs and downstairs men's prayer room. But children can sit anywhere! When I go to the mosque I just run up and down, up and down ... and when grandpa died, in the mosque ...
Sam: Interrupting. He died? How? Did they bury him?
Mehmet: I didn't see the burial but I saw his coffin and he was high up on steps. Maybe that's the steps to heaven.
Daniel: Is it?
Mehmet: Maybe, I don't know.
Daniel: Or he might have rose up to heaven.

Here we have three children sharing a book (a cultural tool) and using it as the starting point for having a discussion. Mehmet, in a sense, is the 'expert' in this session, because the celebration they are looking at is a Turkish one, so the cultural tools and associations are familiar to him. But you can see how Daniel tries to understand the meaning of the steps on which the coffin was placed in terms of his own religious and cultural experience, by suggesting that Mehmet's grandfather might have 'risen to heaven'. Presumably he was thinking of Christianity and the resurrection.

Think about your class or setting and consider whether you offer the following:

- a range of resources which reflect the cultures and languages and experiences of the children in your group;
- opportunities for sharing, collaboration and participation;
- opportunities for the child to be heard and taken seriously;
- opportunities for peer teaching where one child, as the expert, shares knowledge, understanding and experience with others.

Language and concepts: the zone of proximal development

One of the things that should be apparent to you, by now, is the impossibility of discussing one of Vygotsky's ideas without referring to others. We have talked about concepts in the previous section where we related concepts to memory, and to internalisation and to mediation. You will find references to language as a cultural tool in almost everything Vygotsky wrote. Now we will try to draw some of these threads together as we consider one of Vygotsky's most important contributions to *pedagogy*. It is something you are almost certain to have heard of – the zone of proximal development or the ZPD (sometimes referred to as the ZoPeD).

In essence Vygotsky was interested in observing and analysing how children make progress. We have talked about how they move from everyday concepts to scientific concepts, from using cultural tools to enable and enhance memory and then using internalised memory for solving problems. One of the things Vygotsky noted in his last account of the ZPD (to be found in his final work *Thinking and Speech,* 1987[1934]) was that development and instruction (or teaching) do not coincide. *Teaching is only of any benefit to the learner when it moves ahead of development.*

Take a few moments to think about this because it is something very obvious, very important and often largely ignored in many educational programmes and institutions. Teaching is only useful when it moves the learner from where he or she is today to somewhere he or she could be with help. So Vygotsky himself said,

> Instruction is only useful when it moves ahead of development. When it does, it impels or awakens a whole series of functions that are in a stage of maturation lying in development.
>
> (Vygotsky 1987: 212)

By this he meant that when teaching manages to tap into something the child has already experienced, considered or internalised the child is able to move further in terms of thought and problem-solving. The major role of teaching is to do just this and this is what makes the teaching of the human child different from the instruction or training of animals. It is also different from enabling the child to develop a new skill, which can come about through repetition and practice.

Some authors who have written about Vygotsky's work see the ZPD as offering the connection between the spontaneous or everyday concepts that arise through empirical or hands-on learning and the scientific concepts that arise through theoretical or more abstract teaching and learning. There is much debate in the literature about whether this relates to the transmission of knowledge. In fact most authorities agree that Vygotsky was concerned with the broader aspects of learning – things like knowing which tools to use to solve a problem, what techniques and intellectual operations to apply. Here are some examples, all drawn from Smidt (1998) to illustrate this.

Six-year-old Louis was learning his multiplication tables and the teacher taught him what he called 'a trick' for working out the 9 times table. For a week he spent much of his time with paper, pencil and calculator and then told his childminder, Maria Figueiredo, what he had discovered:

Louis: Imagine you are doing 5 × 4. Now 4 is an even number, so for even numbers you break them into half and then add a zero to the number. See?

He held up the paper to me so I could see his work:

$$5 \times 4 = ?$$
$$4 / 2 = 2$$
$$= 20$$

Louis: Now listen carefully because the odd numbers are harder. Imagine we are doing 5 × 3. Three is the number you are going to work on, so this time you go for the number which comes before 3 which is 2. Then break it into half, which is 1 and add a 5 to it which makes 15!

(Figueiredo 1998: 39)

This is a wonderful example of a child being able to explain, in some detail, the solution to a problem he set himself through what he had learned through formal instruction at school. He identified the problem and used tools including mathematical symbols (=, ×, /) and language – the latter both to explain the problem and its solution, and, as a tool for his thinking paper, pencil and calculator. It is questionable whether he would ever have had the opportunity in class to reveal just how much he knew. A teacher with the pressures and demands of many children to attend to might never find the time to invite this sort of exchange.

> A four-year-old girl is looking at a collection of shells, rocks and pebbles, untidily arranged on a table with an assortment of magnifiers of different shapes and sizes. She selects one large spiral shell and examines it closely, first with the naked eye and then with some of the magnifiers. She uses the hand lenses, large and small, moving them to and fro to get the best magnification. She bends down and puts her face right up against the lens, as if she is trying to work out the best distance between her eyes, the lens and the shell. Then she puts the shell down on the table, placing it under the magnifying glass mounted on a tripod; she leans over the tripod, satisfied she has seen all there is to see. Then she puts the shell back on the table, under the tripod, and bends over it once more, laying her ear close to the lens, as if she were listening to the shell, through the magnifying glass.
>
> (Drummond 1998: 103)

This observation is fascinating in terms of how clearly it allows us to follow the processes this little girl goes through as she explores some objects available to her in a school environment. The educators have provided interesting natural objects together with the tools to allow further physical exploration. There is no evidence of any spoken language in this extract and the reader is left to fill in the possible thoughts going through that child's mind as she moved from one thing to another. Most fascinating is her assumption that a tool (the magnifying glass), which she realised could make things *look* bigger, might be able to make the same things *sound* louder.

Neither of the two examples makes any reference to adults involved in interaction with the children. Yet Vygotsky assures us that *all learning is social*, and when reading those examples and often when seeing what children do in your setting *you have to infer the social from what takes place*. What is important in the ZPD is the notion of *potential*. What the child does when engaged in a task is what the child reveals she knows and can do today: potential refers to what the child might be able to do with help. The gap between the two is the ZPD. So the role of the adult or more expert learner is clear. It is to help the child move from the *performance* level to the *potential* level.

You will probably have come across the term '*scaffolding*'. This is often used to refer to the role of the more expert other in helping the child move from the performance level to the potential level. Some writers describe the help that the more expert learner should give as being like the scaffolding which holds up a building under construction, which is only removed once the building is complete. So the support offered is thought of as small, supporting steps.

Here is an example of an adult scaffolding a child's learning drawn from a small observation made by Susan Bragg (1998). Louisa was involved in making things at the 'making table'. She started off with a plan she had drawn and then went in search of the resources she had decided she needed:

> as she walked over to the wood she said to herself 'Now what bit do I need?' Taking a long piece of wood in her other hand she returned to her seat. She placed the wood on the table, saying, 'This is big enough,' and then emptied the beads out of her hand onto the table. Next she took the glue and squeezed little blobs of it along the wood …
>
> (Bragg 1998: 143–5)

She carried on in this way, talking the process aloud and showing her work in progress to the other children. Then she needed something to stick two pieces of wood together. First she remembered the glue gun and asked the adult to help her with that. But it didn't work. Then she decided to attach some foam to a piece of wood, but the glue gun did not work on that either. *Noticing that Louisa was getting frustrated the adult suggested using an elastic band.*

> 'Good. It worked!' she said, looking at the other children. 'That's good, isn't it, using an elastic band?'

The consequence of that small but focused intervention was to allow Louisa to work for 45 minutes to make her 'boat' and fulfil her plans. She was delighted!

In this example the scaffolding needed was minimal but it required that the adult involved pay close attention to the child, understand what the child was doing and identify what help the child needed. This is a highly skilled thing to do and needs close and sensitive observation – not brash intervention which risks interfering with the child's agenda.

There are a number of difficulties in using the term 'scaffolding'. One is that there is a danger of seeing scaffolding as a one-way process in which the scaffolder is in charge and 'presents' learning to the novice. This is the blank slate or empty vessel view of learning which was certainly not that of Vygotsky. Others (Newman *et al.* 1989) insist that the ZPD is constructed through negotiation between the more expert learner and the novice. The question then arises as to where the support from the more expert learner comes from. Vygotsky appears not to have addressed this issue. Moll (1990) thinks that the process that takes place in the ZPD should be about collaboration, enhancement and communication of meaning rather than about transfer of skills or knowledge.

What do we learn from this?

Vygotsky's work on the social nature of learning and the importance of mediation and cultural tools leads inevitably to the concept of the ZPD. For us it entails that we do the following:

- Ensure that the scientific concepts we want to teach are built on a sound foundation of spontaneous or everyday activities. Mathematics, science, technology and other areas of knowledge have been socially constructed and children cannot come to understanding these without extensive experience at the everyday level. In other words, children need first-hand or concrete experience before they can deal with theoretical or abstract concepts.
- Know as much as possible about what experience each child has had, including languages spoken and/or understood, cultural tools, values and expectations.
- Take time to observe children, listen to them and talk to them.
- Take time to think about what each observation you make tells you, not in order to tick a box on a checklist but in order to know more about what it is that the child is trying to do or say or make or understand.
- Take their ideas and theories seriously and invite children to tell you about them and to ask you questions that arise in their heads.
- Intervene sensitively, appropriately, taking your lead from the child and not appropriating the child's agenda.
- Keep documents and records of what children say and do so that you build a dynamic and meaningful picture of what each child is learning.

Scaffolding and peer tutoring

Vygotsky's thoughts on moving the learner from the actual to the possible have been influential in many learning institutions in many countries throughout the world. Called different things at different times, the idea, in summary, is that a more expert learner alongside a novice learner, paying attention to what the child is doing or saying, can provide some support to help the child achieve what is just out of reach. Whether this is called scaffolding or cognitive apprenticeship, reciprocal teaching, peer tutoring or situated learning, all share roots with this idea. As you read through the definitions below you might like to think about whether any or all of them offer you suggestions for organising your teaching.

- *Cognitive apprenticeships* are naturally situated within the social constructivist paradigm. Constructivists see learners as being active constructors of meaning rather than passive recipients of knowledge. In this model learners work collaboratively on projects or problems with the close scaffolding of the instructor. The tasks should be slightly more difficult than the learners could manage independently, requiring the help of either their peers or an adult or both to succeed. One of the key features of those who advocate this 'variant' is that learners should not be working alone.
- *Situated learning* is so called because it is based on the concept that learning as it normally occurs is a function of the activity itself and of the context and the culture in which it occurs (which means that it is situated). Beyond the early years most classrooms involve learning activities which are primarily abstract and out of context. We know that social interaction is a critical component of situated learning: learners become involved in what some writers call a '*community of practice*', a group of learners sharing a set of beliefs and values. As the novice moves from the periphery of this community to its centre, he or she becomes more active and more engaged with the culture, adopting its beliefs and values. After a while she is able to assume the role of expert.
- *Reciprocal teaching* most commonly refers to an instructional activity that takes place as a dialogue between teachers and students regarding segments of text. It is most usually applied to language lessons or classes, and the dialogue is structured by the use of four strategies. These are summarising, question-generating, clarifying and predicting, and you can see from this that it could be applied to any subject area or body of knowledge. What makes the teaching reciprocal is that the teacher and students take turns assuming the role of teacher in leading the dialogue.
- *Peer tutoring* is defined by Damon and Phelps as 'an approach in which one child instructs another child in material on which the first is an expert and the second is a novice' (1989: 11). Not all writers on peer tutoring accept this definition, some insisting that the peers need to be roughly the same age. However, if you read the work of Kenner (2004a) you will realise that while

some of the children involved in this are of similar ages what is common to them all is that one of the pair is an expert in something whereas the other is a novice. So perhaps the definition better reflects this than similarity in ages.

Looking back, looking ahead

In this chapter we have looked back at what was said in the first four chapters and have tried to draw out the implications for us as practitioners. Clearly, with such a strong emphasis on both the social and cultural, much of what we have thought about is how to create learning environments which both reflect the cultures, languages and other cultural tools of the children and also offer activities which allow children to build on their previous experience through extending their range of everyday concepts. We continue to stress the importance in learning of interaction between children and children or between children and adults. And we insist that for children to be able to acquire scientific concepts they first need a sound foundation of everyday concepts. We looked at the ZPD and thought about the role of educators in helping children bridge the gap between what they can do alone and what they might do after being helped. This led us to consider scaffolding and the varieties of ways in which this has been interpreted.

In the next chapter we will begin to consider what some writers are calling activity theory. We also take a very brief look at the work of some of those who were influenced by Vygotsky's work and used, adapted or critiqued it.

Glossary

Word or phrase	What it means	Why it is significant
cognitive apprenticeship	Another way of describing scaffolding where the learner works alongside others and can watch and learn from them.	Another term to describe scaffolding.
community of practice	This refers to a group of people who share values or beliefs.	The people who provide the models for learners and to whose group they eventually belong. This has implications for teachers who group children.

genetic laws	Vygotsky devised a set of laws related to how experience was mediated through interaction.	Vygotsky's genetic laws are his explanation for learning and are significant for us.
in-growth	This refers to the move from thinking without to thinking within. An example is when things become internalised.	Part of Vygotsky's genetic laws
peer tutoring	This is where one learner adopts the role of expert in teaching another learner.	A teaching tool that allows both partners, novice and expert, to learn more.
reciprocal teaching	This term usually refers to a teaching activity which is set in the form of a dialogue between teachers and students.	More appropriate for older children.
scaffolding	A term used by Bruner to explain what more expert others could do to provide carefully scaled support to enable children to bridge the zone of proximal development.	Essential to those of us wanting to explore ways of helping learners become independent thinkers.
situated learning	This refers to the notion that learning is a function of the activity itself and that the context and culture are vital to it.	The importance of this is that it reminds us that the activities themselves are important in determining what is learned and how it is learned.
sociogenesis	This refers to the transition from social to individual forms of behaviour – or from learning with people to being able to do things alone.	Part of Vygotsky's genetic laws.
transition	Synonymous with mediation, it means the move from natural forms of behaviour to cultural forms of behaviour	Part of Vygotsky's genetic laws.

Chapter 6

Activity theory

In this chapter we turn our attention to what is known as activity theory and in doing this go over some ground we have already covered as well as introducing some new thoughts and ideas. We start by looking at how and why the theory arose, and then move on to examine the ideas of people who were influenced by Vygotsky's work and went on either to develop it further or to criticise it in the light of what has been learned since his work was first published in English. Activity theory is currently being much promoted and debated. In essence activity theory can be defined as being synonymous with sociocultural theory but with the emphasis placed on activity itself, whereas the emphasis in sociocultural theory is on mediation.

The development of activity theory

The *cultural-historical theory of activity* (to give it its full name) was formulated by our friends Vygotsky, Luria and Leontiev in Russia during the 1920s and 1930s. It arose from Vygotsky's dissatisfaction with approaches to psychology at the time, which were dominated by what he regarded as two unsatisfactory orientations – psychoanalysis and behaviourism. In order to overcome this he and his colleagues arrived at a new theoretical construct: the double-edged ideas of *artefact-mediated* and *object-oriented* action. Artefact-mediated means something that happens through the use of cultural tools and object-oriented refers to opportunities for first-hand exploration or concrete experience. For Vygotsky a human individual never reacts directly to the environment. Rather, all relationships between a human being and objects or events in the environment are mediated by cultural means, tools and signs. For example, language is used through interactions between child and adult as a means of communication and sharing of attention. Then language is internalised by means of the child's thinking and control of her activity.

There is a simple diagram to illustrate this, which is known as the *first generation* of activity theory; it is a triangle which shows the links between the subject, the object and the mediating tool (Fig. 6.1). An activity is made up of a subject and an object, mediated by a tool. The subject is a person or a group of people engaged in the activity, and the object is what the subject is interested in or

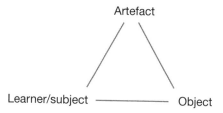

Figure 6.1 The first generation of activity theory

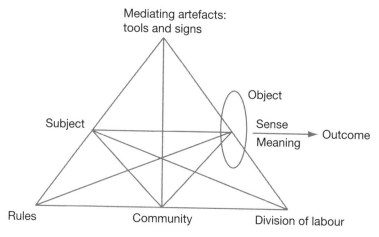

Figure 6.2 Second-generation activity theory model. Adapted from Engeström 1987

exploring and is what gives the activity its drive or its direction. The mediation can take place though many symbolic, cultural or material tools.

A *second generation* of the theory arose through the later work of Leontiev who looked at the activity of work and at how the tools involved in *joint collective action* mediate socially. The diagram which illustrates this (Fig. 6.2) is more complex, involving links between the learner and object, the learner and community, the learner and tools, the learner and rules and then links between others, including the division of labour. You may find this difficult to interpret but one of the things you might learn from it is that the object, which is represented in this version by an oval shape, is meant to show how object-oriented actions are always open to different interpretations and carry the potential for change.

Leontiev believed that he had to separate individual action (what an individual does on her own) from collective activity (what people do when they work together). So the distinction between activity, action and operation was added to the definition. Read the example below which will help you to understand what this means:

> When members of a tribe are hunting they individually have separate goals and they are in charge of diverse actions. Some are frightening a herd of animals towards other hunters who kill the game, and other members have other tasks. These actions have immediate goals, but the real motive is beyond hunting. Together these people aim at obtaining food and clothing – at staying alive. To understand why separate actions are meaningful one needs to understand the motive behind the whole activity. Activity is guided by a motive.
>
> (Leontiev 1978: 62–3)

This is something worth bearing in mind when children or other learners are working as a group. Individuals may well be involved in different actions but the group must share a common goal for the event to be regarded as an activity. Engeström (1999) developed the original triangular representation of activity systems to allow for an exploration of systems of activity at the macro level, which, you will remember, refers to the collective and community levels beyond the micro levels described by Bronfenbrenner. By expanding the original triangular representation of Figure 6.1 to the one in Figure 6.2 he aims to show the social/collective elements in the activity system while adding to it things like the division of labour (the work/jobs people do in society), community and rules.

Michael Cole noticed that the first two generations of activity theory were insensitive to cultural diversity and devised a *third generation* with an even more complicated diagram. Too complicated to include here, it involves the development of conceptual tools to understand dialogue, multiple perspectives and voices, and networks of interacting activity systems. Engeström also studied a third generation of activity theory but his interest arose out of his work with students, whom he saw as collectives of learners. One of the problems in doing this is that the subject (or the learner) is not always the same person. In a collective activity the learner at one point in time might not be the learner at the next point. He also felt that goals are associated with actions and hence with individuals and cannot be attached to the activity as a whole. In his words:

> Activity is achieved through constant negotiation, orchestration and struggle between different goals and perspectives of its participants. The object and motive of a collective activity are something like a constantly evolving mosaic, a pattern that is never completed.
>
> (Engeström 1999, cited in Daniels 2001: 90)

Kearney (2003) provides a very moving account of the experiences of young adults from different ethnic and cultural groups while on a degree course in Community Theatre Arts. In the second year the students were invited to form their own groups and Aliki, a Greek speaker, tells of her shock when the white students formed a group without any discussion with the others. You need to hear her voice to feel the impact of this:

> The people who were left was me, my Asian friend Luna, my African friend Zande, my Asian friend Kaken and my West Indian friend, Cherry. And they were all the black, Greek, Asian people in our year ... and we hadn't even spoken to each other ... (about the project). And every one piped up and said 'Oh, that's great ... you can form a group and do something about (laughs) minority groups ...'
> [...] We were all in this room, I said, 'I think it's disgusting. I've not got a chip on my shoulder about being Greek and if I have then, OK fine, but look there's white people over there and there's all us bloody ethnics over here. If we're a Community Theatre Arts Course and we're trying to represent sections of the community that aren't represented in theatre, then why are we all together and you guys are all over there?'
>
> (Kearney 2003: 120)

Aliki goes on to tell how ineffectual the tutors were, and how she felt the lack of a role model was serious. Her solution was to write her own play, using her own experience to construct her own identity. We see here a group of children who are part of a larger group and encounter the discouragement, ambivalence and lack of shared understandings in what is described as a collective and collaborative experience. There is no direct link with activity theory here: this account has been included in order to illustrate just how important it is that issues regarding diversity be part of any analysis.

Engeström (1987) developed a set of five principles related to the current state of activity theory. They read like this:

1 The first principle reminds us of the fact that a *collective*, object-oriented, and artefact-mediated activity system is the prime unit of analysis although it can be linked in a network to other such systems.
2 The second principle talks about how *multi-voiced* activity systems are. You came across an example of this in the extract from Chris Kearney's book about the students on the Community Arts Project, which is all about voice. So any activity is made up of different points of view, traditions and interests.
3 The third principle is that activities are always *situated in a history* and need to be understood in terms of their history.
4 The fourth principle is one which highlights the fact that *contradictions are sources of change and development* and play a central role in activities.
5 And the last principle is one that suggests that *transformations and change are made possible through activity systems*.

The Fifth Dimension after-school programme

Duncan and Tarulli (2003) argue that activity theory can be regarded as Vygotsky's way of defining stages of development. Unlike Piaget (who thought human beings progressed through clear stages according to age), Vygotsky considered that stages were not fixed according to age but were more *ecological* in origin. You will remember that ecological means the relationships of groups in society and their environment. They talk of *leading activities*, by which they mean *activities which focus on changes or transitions in the child's position within society*. So a transition from home to school makes a change of position as does a change from school to work and so on. Accompanying each such change in position is a corresponding change in psychological processes. You will have noticed how transitions (the entry to school or setting, changing class or school, the arrival of a new baby) all change the child's position and are accompanied by varying emotional changes – anxiety, happiness, alienation and so on. These, in their turn, may affect motivation and there are claims that this can create new zones of proximal development.

Michael Cole was interested in how cultural historical activity theory (CHAT) could be used to design after-school education activity systems (Cole and Distributed Literacy Consortium 1996). There were several reasons for doing this – to improve educational standards, to provide a safe place for children to be after school, and in response to proposed reforms of higher education in the USA. Their solution was to propose the Fifth Dimension, an educational activity system which offers school-aged children a specially designed environment in which to explore off-the-shelf computer games and game-like educational activities after school hours. (You will see the link to Vygotsky more clearly when you have read the chapter which follows this.) The computer games are part of a make-believe world that includes other games and artefacts. Special instruction cards are written by staff to make the games accessible to the participants and these provide opportunities to think about and criticise information, or to write to someone, or look up information or to teach someone else what has been learned – a range of social exchanges and interactions, involving the use of cultural tools. There is also an electronic entity, a wizard or a wizardess who is said to live in the internet and who writes to or chats with children via the internet. In the mythology of the Fifth Dimension this creature acts as the patron of the participants, the provider of games, the mediator of disputes and the solver of computer and other problems.

Within a centre where a Fifth Dimension programme is based, there will be someone who welcomes the children and supervises the flow of activity, who is trained to support the pedagogical foundations of the programme. Also based in the centre are university and college students. They are enrolled on a course focusing on fieldwork in community settings. Cole states that the Fifth Dimension has been organised so as to create an institutional version of the zone of proximal development for the participants. The more expert others may not always be those you expect: you may find a child who is more skilled at playing computer games than a university student, for example. But there is a culture of collaborative learning. Cole also reminds us that each Fifth Dimension site is different, influenced by its own history and that of its community, by the cultural tools used and the changing resources available.

There are some underpinning principles involved in each one, however, one of which is the importance of *joint mediated activity* which is embedded in a set of nested contexts: child, students and computer in a club; the club in the neighbourhood; the neighbourhood in a school district which channels children into the club; then a community whose children are served by the school district, and so on. Picture this as a series of concentric circles with the club at the centre and you will appreciate what he means. In a sense Cole uses the term activity to replace context; he says it is useful to think of the Fifth Dimension activity system as being made up of several different elements – the interplay of subjects or learners with their objectives or goals; mediational tools, like language or other symbolic systems; social rules; and the division of labour

The system is rule-bound and in some of the sites games are presented in the form of a maze, through which the learners make their way in negotiation with the wizard. The wizard also invites them to reflect on their own learning and progress. There are different levels of task and the child can decide the sequence. Completion of a passage through the maze allows the child the possibility to become a wizard's assistant who can support others and in doing that extend their own learning. So the Fifth Dimension seeks to promote collaborative learning within a system of shared rules. And the play within the maze is play with rules.

Looking at leading activity and discourse guides

Mercer (2000) wanted to try to apply some of Cole's findings and thoughts to participation inside schools, focusing here on the *leading activity* of school. He is interested in how children think and become able to appropriate collective thinking – the thinking of others in their culture or cultures. He talks of *interthinking* and was influenced also by the work of Lave and Wenger (1991), who, in their turn, were influenced by Rogoff's work on guided participation. The thesis is that more experienced and more expert members of communities can act as '*discourse guides*' and in classrooms these will often be teachers or other practitioners. Mercer identified the characteristics of what he defined as effective teachers:

1 They are teachers who *use question and answer session not merely to test knowledge but also to guide the development of understanding.*

Vivian Gussin Paley has written many books on the role of storytelling, talk and honesty in education. Here is an extract from her book *The Kindness of Children* (1999). As a storyteller she visits many groups, telling stories, offering starting points for pretend play and listening to the children's contributions. In the brief extract below we find her in a Californian fourth grade classroom where the talk is getting very emotional.

> 'My uncle thinks a person needs to be alone sometimes,' Luis says. 'He tells my brothers, "Let Luis do this by himself, you guys make him too sad". He used to do that to our father, see, he made him too sad, and he's sorry, and now it's too late.'
> 'Do you listen to your uncle, Luis?'
> 'Yeah, we're nicer when he's there …'
> 'What would your uncle do about Harry?' I ask and Luis answers so promptly it is clear he and his uncle speak of such things. 'He'd figure out if Harry is sad, you know, maybe his father is dead or he's in jail, something bad. Let him have a breather, that's what my uncle says. A breather. You know, let him be happy now, and then later he'll make you happy.' Luis's words have great meaning for his classmates, most of whom know his uncle, a teacher in the school.
>
> (Paley 1999: 14–15)

2   They are teachers who *focus not only on the subject context but also offer suggestions for the ways in which problems can be solved and meanings made and shared.*

Here is an example to illustrate this. Mary Smith, working in a Children's Centre, was involved with a group of children, one of whom became interested in some bees in the garden and wanted to make honey. My comments and explications are in square brackets and are given to point out the problem-solving strategies she is offering Daniel throughout the interaction.

> He said we could make some honey at the nursery. I asked him how we could do it. [She is inviting him to consider what he thinks before telling him what to do.]
> He replied that we had to pick some flowers together. We went inside to get a tray for the flowers, then back to the garden to collect wild flowers – daisies, buttercups and dandelions. When the tray was full we sat on the grass and studied them. Daniel said, 'We have to pick out the pollen from the centre of each flower.' It took a while to do this, placing it in the corner of the tray. Daniel said we had enough to make the honey and then asked me to get a cup and spoon. I got them. Daniel put the contents into the cup and then stirred it with the spoon saying, 'I know it will make honey!'
> After a time I asked, 'What's happening to it, Daniel?' [Asking him a question to encourage him to make an assessment of what has happened and to suggest a solution.] 'Nothing,' he replied. 'We have to add apple juice to

it and then it will be honey.' I got the apple juice from the kitchen. Daniel poured it into the cup and stirred, saying, 'Is it honey now?'

'No,' I replied. 'I don't think people can make honey ... only bees.' Daniel was not convinced and said, 'We have to put more pollen in and then it will be honey.' [She followed Daniel's lead and was not tempted to just tell him he was wrong.] We added more, but couldn't make honey. At this point I said, 'Daniel, we've tried our best to make honey, but people can't make it. We'll look for a book about bees and that will show us how they make it.' [She showed him how books and other tools can be used when first-hand experience fails to solve a problem.]

We found a book and sat for a long time reading, looking and explaining – page by page. As a follow-up we went to the shop to buy honey and even managed to get a jar with honeycomb in it. [She ensured that there was a positive outcome so that the child did not experience a sense of failure.] The children enjoyed the experience of spreading the honey on rolls and eating them at tea time.

(Smith 1998: 148-9)

3 They are teachers who *treat learning as a social and communicative process*.

Both of the examples cited earlier illustrate teachers who do this and here is another example from the work of the late Josie Levine. This is a powerful and moving account of what took place in one of her classes – a 'reception class' in a secondary school which was full-time and all-age and designed for newly arrived immigrant children who had yet to learn English. She notes that there were advantages in that they were able to build their own classroom culture. Here is her moving account of one classroom interaction:

> Gurnak is one of those who call for quiet when Biro and Kabel tell their troubles in this way. He is more explicit about what is going on inside and outside the classroom. The windows of his house brick-broken for the second time, he asks bitter questions. 'What for they do this thing, Miss? My father good man, my mother good woman. Work hard. No make trouble.' And on another day when I am lecturing about how they should behave, he challenges me. 'Miss, why you tell us be good all the time? I *am* good boy, Miss. Why I must be gooder than English boy? Why you tell me this, Miss? Where is fair?' I cannot answer. I am shocked to discover how much of what I resented as a kid but could not articulate, I am unquestioningly asking of them. [...] Gurnak's question reveals to me that I do not know what to do to act against the racism on the streets, despite the fact that some twenty years before we too had hate and stones thrown at us by other children as we left our (Jewish) school for home each day.

(Levine, in Meek 1996: 30)

This is a real and serious dialogue between two partners who are equal in the discussion and who hear one another with attention and respect. It is a way of building trust between learner and teacher, in this case.

After Vygotsky: Levine and Bakhtin

Vygotsky, writing in the early part of the last century in Russia, was certainly not considering linguistic and cultural diversity but many people who have read and been influenced by his work have applied much of it to working in a more globalised and multicultural world. Josie Levine, whose work you have just encountered and who worked in multilingual classrooms throughout her sadly short career, believed that such classrooms could only benefit all learners if they were built on partnerships. These would include children learning from and with one another in small groups or pairs; teachers working in partnership with pupils; and teachers planning and working together to support pupils' learning. This is an approach built on providing language-rich classrooms; the sharing of attention and purpose; acknowledging the histories and experiences of the participants; learning dialectically (which means considering different and sometimes opposing points of view); and being active in deciding what and how and with whom to learn. The approach she was advocating was called *developmental pedagogy* and this is a phrase that has gone out of fashion (as has a real concern to maintain the diversity in our rich society). Levine draws our attention to the fact that Vygotsky did refer to learning 'foreign' languages in some of his writing and in his later writing – in *Thinking and Speech*, the 1987 edition of *Thought and Language* (1962) – he suggests that disembedded teaching of a second or additional language may not be successful, despite it being the kind of teaching he believed was essential to learning higher order concepts. He did recognise the cognitive benefits that come from knowing more than one language: learners who have acquired a second language are able to reflect on their own language and on the structure of the language they have learned.

Bakhtin (1979) shared with Vygotsky the view that human consciousness arises through the interplay between our internal consciousness and the external forces which act upon us, mediated by socially constructed cultural tools. It is important to remember that consciousness means awareness of something. Bakhtin and Vygotsky were concerned with inner and outer, internal and external. Bakhtin, however, challenged some of Vygotsky's ideas and did so in a way which offers us much to think about. He was very aware of the nature of our society and used the term *heteroglossia* to describe the linguistic and ideological diversity of cultural life. When he considered Vygotsky's notion of appropriation of culture or of language he felt that the situation was more complex and nuanced than one might first think. He believed that cultures, in general, were not unified but rather were made up of competing and contrasting values and views of the world. We have thought about how children begin to appropriate concepts, language, roles and rules through their interactions. Bakhtin thinks that this is not simply appropriation whereby the learner adopts, without question, what they are appropriating. Everything that learners are involved in carries with it the following:

- possibilities of disagreement;
- difference; and
- possibilities for shared meanings and understandings.

For Bakhtin the social world is characterised by the struggles of the many social languages of heteroglossia and so is the child's playground and play world. This is complicated but in essence Bakhtin is arguing that for a child to become who she will be more is involved than just internalising the thoughts and ideas of others. It involves *engaging in some inner discourse with these ideas, and choosing which to accept while rejecting those that are not acceptable.* This is how children are able to find an individual identity and a particular and unique voice. This is something you might find interesting and relevant and it is certainly something that is being studied by various researchers today.

In her book on gender, Blaise (2005) shows how children, having acquired appropriate cultural norms around gender, struggle to overcome the realities of life when they conflict with these norms. In an issue related to boys and strength Blaise describes how she was in a school observing five- and six-year-old children climbing up a rope. She noticed that some of the boys – Keith, Ian, Liam and James – were unable to reach the top of the rope. Here is an extract from her observation notes:

> At first it appears that as the children climb the rope they are being cheered on and encouraged by their classmates. However, I discover that the cheering is not the same for everyone. That is, when a girl fails to reach the ceiling and then slides down the rope, her friends console her with pats on the back while shaking their heads, coupled with comments such as 'Good job', 'Better luck next time' and 'Oh, it's okay'. However, when a boy is unable to reach the top of the rope and returns to the blue mat he is ignored …
>
> […] Alan quietly and intensely watches as more girls successfully reach the top of the rope and touch the ceiling. The girls are consistently outperforming the boys, confronting his notion of how the world is and should be … Incidentally, Alan is one of the only two boys who can climb to the top of the rope.
>
> (Blaise 2005: 103)

In a classroom discussion that follows Blaise asks the children who the strongest in the class is and Alan responds by citing the names of three boys. Blaise then asks which are the three strongest girls and Alan's response is, 'Nobody', while he looks her straight in the eyes, suggesting this is a ridiculous question. Despite repeated questions and reminders of the names of the girls who had succeeded where the boys had not, Alan rigidly sticks to his guns.

He then insists that girls cannot be strong because they don't have 'big, big, big muscles'.

Looking back, looking ahead

In this chapter we have looked at activity theory – the name given to aspects of Vygotsky's work – and tracked its development over what are called three generations. We have also seen how Michael Cole, an expert on the work of Vygotsky who has been very involved in translating and interpreting his work, took activity theory as a model for work he introduced in the USA to offer learning opportunities in after-school settings. That led us to look at the work of other researchers and theorists and we ended up taking a very brief look at the work of Michael Bakhtin, who helps us understand the struggle we may have to accommodate conflicting views.

In the next chapter we turn our attention to play and meaning. This is an important chapter in this book so do take your time in reading it.

Glossary

Word or phrase	What it means	Why it is significant
artefact-mediated	Means through the use of cultural tools.	Practitioners need to be aware of the fact that much learning comes about through the use of cultural tools and ensure that those offered are appropriate to the learner.
collective	A term used to describe groups of learners working together and collaboratively.	A model of teaching we are used to, although it is important for children, especially younger children, to also have time to be in small groups or to be alone.
cultural-historical theory of activity	A theory of learning based on an analysis of the role of experience in learning over time and with reference to culture.	Practitioners will need to be alert to knowing as much as possible about the past life and experiences of the children in their care.

developmental pedagogy	Josie Levine's theory of good pedagogy which allows for partnership between learners and teachers, genuine and participatory dialogue and being active in devising the what and how of learning.	Practitioners will want to ensure that the classrooms and settings in which they work are places which buzz with talk.
discourse guide	Another term of Mercer's to describe those he regarded as more expert others – often teachers or other practitioners.	Practitioners might want to think about the possible discourses available through interactions between learners and more expert others.
ecological	Ecological is a term you have encountered before with regard to the work of Bronfenbrenner and it describes how things are related to their environment and influences from close to remote.	This is something we have mentioned earlier in this book.
heteroglossia	Bakhtin's term to describe the diverse nature of social life, thinking about the range of languages and ideas embedded in all cultures.	Another reminder of the need to move from a dominant to an inclusive approach to all education.
interthinking	A term used by Mercer to refer to how he believed learners were able to appropriate or take on the learning of their culture. Sometimes criticised for not being sensitive enough to children being able to inhabit several worlds at the same time.	Practitioners should be alert to evidence that children are taking on and using the learning of their culture.

joint mediated activity	A term used by Cole to discuss his programme for after-school establishments and referring to how a child is set in a web of things – an activity in a centre in a neighbourhood in a school district and so on.	The Fifth Dimension is interesting and certainly contains some issues of use to all educators.
leading activity	Part of Vygotsky's theory of development and learning, these were conceived of as the main areas or domains in which learning took place. Play was the first and regarded as the leading activity pre-school. School and work followed.	An interesting theory but perhaps rather too broad to be of practical use to us. For me it does not allow for a more detailed and sensitive approach to learning within the very broad span of schooling from early years onwards.
multi-voiced	How different perspectives, attitudes, views and needs are catered for. It is easy to think about this in terms of each child's voice being heard and paid attention to.	Another reminder to hear the voices of the children and ensure they are allowed to keep them.
object-oriented	When applied to activity or experience this refers to the role of the concrete.	Reminds us of the need to offer meaningful and concrete experiences to learners before engaging them in abstract thinking.

Chapter 7

On play and meaning

In this chapter we turn our attention to something with which you are very familiar – namely play. And we start, as we often do, by defining what we mean by – on this occasion – play. (Please note: in this chapter there is a running attempt to define what we mean by play and definitions are added as we cover more material. You will see what this means as you read the chapter.)

It is essential to do this because play is an everyday word which refers to many different things. We talk of playing the fool, playing the trumpet, playing at being older, playing football, playing Monopoly, playing truant and so on. Each of those phrases refers to a slightly different meaning for the word. The play that we do when we play the fool is not the same as the play we do when we play the trumpet. And since play has a very specific meaning when used by educationalists it is important that when we talk about it here we start from a shared meaning. If you ask people for their everyday definitions of play these will often include the words 'pleasure', 'fun', 'non-serious' and so on. If you ask educationalists for their more 'scientific' definitions of play these are likely to focus on the words 'self-chosen', 'risk-free' and 'engaging'. For our purposes let us agree the three points below to act as baseline definitions which we may change before the end of this chapter:

Definition 1   Play is self-chosen and allows the child to follow her own agenda in order to address her needs or interests. So when a child chooses to play in the home corner and chooses what to do within that play, what we see is real play. When the child goes into the home corner because it is her turn or because someone has told her to, this is not play.

Definition 2   Play is risk-free in the sense that if things don't go according to plan the plan can change since the child is in charge. So there is no possibility of failure.

Definition 3   Because the child has chosen to play, the play itself is deeply engaging and involving and can last for a few seconds or over days or even weeks. It can be solitary or involve others. Often, but not always, it involves an imaginary world in which signs and symbols may play a part.

You may notice that there is no mention of 'social' or 'cultural' or 'interaction' or 'tools' or 'feelings' in these definitions so we will surely have to attend to this before the end of the chapter.

Tina Bruce (1991), in a section in her book called 'Theories of play', talks of play as *preparation for life* or as an *integrating mechanism*. With the latter term she is thinking of the ways in which, in play, children bring together, integrate and use their existing knowledge and understanding. Her own preference is for what she calls *free-flow play* – a term that was popular for a time – and which she defined as when children wallow in ideas, feelings and relationships while they apply the competence and technical prowess they have already developed. So play for Bruce is clearly social, clearly involves feelings and clearly builds on and extends experience through the use of cultural tools. We will return to this when we start to unpick Vygotsky's ideas on play later in this chapter.

It is important to note that in the developed Western world play has been given almost mythical status by educators who – sometimes without fully understanding just why play might be important as a learning mechanism – state that it is *the* most significant way in which young children learn. This has been assisted by the growth of consumerism so that young parents are seduced into spending vast sums of money on what are claimed to be 'educational' toys, and settings and centres are often more concerned with their equipment than with their practice. Play is certainly important in the lives of most children and they certainly learn and consolidate through play. But they also learn through their everyday interactions and rituals – such as going to the hospital to have a cut stitched, cooking chapattis, being out in the fields alongside their working parents, eating, walking to school, watching television, listening to stories told or read, and so on.

Children seem to play in all cultures throughout the world. They start by exploring their physical world by using movement and their senses. They pick up and examine objects. They put them in their mouths. They drop them and pick them up. They shake them. Because the child is not engaged in an overtly social activity and is not using spoken language we may be tempted to consider this as experimental play without thought or meaning. But, the question arises, is this so? (This is where the numbered definitions continue.)

Adding to our definition of play

Definition 4   Although play may be solitary it is almost certainly social in origin in that the child will often play out events they have experienced with others. Interaction with others is often, although not always, part of play.

Definition 5   Play is mediated by cultural tools such as signs and symbols, and toys and other objects, and, of course, by language.

Definition 6   In play children, since they control the play, can express, in safety, their fears, anger, joy, jealousy or other feelings. So there is an affective element to play.

Play and meaning

For Vygotsky play was an activity different from other children's activities in the sense that in playing the child creates 'pretend play' situations – a concept with which we are all familiar. Our definition of play certainly includes pretend play, but is not limited to it. What Vygotsky says is that the child is able to engage in pretend play because the child is able to start to separate the visual field from the field of sense, or meaning. This makes play a step in the *decontextualisation of meaning* – the ability to think about something even when the thing is not present or evident. When a young child explores an object the child uses perception and this involves examining not only the colour or shape or size or texture of the object but also its meaning. It is as though the child asks the question (implicitly, of course), 'What is this thing?' Vygotsky talks about this as *the child being able to separate the visual field (what can be seen) from the field of sense (what can be implied) and sees this as the first step on the road to the development of higher mental functions and of verbal thinking*. This makes explicit the role that play has in cognitive or intellectual development.

More than this, in play the ability of the child to take charge of her own activity begins. Any pretend play situation involves a rule if we define 'rule' as a specific principle to which the child adjusts. It is important to understand that such a rule is not set by someone else but comes about through the meaning the child has attributed to the object. In Vygotsky's own words:

> It seems to me that one can put forward a statement that whenever a child does not follow the rules, whenever he does not specifically adjust to the rules, one cannot speak of play at all. [...] we have managed to demonstrate that every 'pretend play' situation includes hidden rules [...] and every play with rules contains 'pretend play' situations in a concealed form.
> (1962, cited in Bruner *et al.* 1976: 73–5)

Read through these vignettes to see if you can find the hidden rule.

1   *A piece of wood becomes, in the child's mind, a wand.*
    The rules the child attributes to wands must then be applied. They can be waved. They create magic. The child has arrived at these rules through interaction and experience.

2   *A building block becomes a mobile phone.*
    The rules applying to mobile phones must be applied. They must be held to the ear and one speaks into them or one holds them up in the air and uses them to take a photograph.

3   *The child plays at being the mother in the home corner.*
    The child becomes the mother. The rules of 'being mother' apply. The child must be in charge, be loving, or be angry in accordance with the mothering the child has experienced, or with a feeling or set of feelings the child needs to explore.

The child, in using one object or situation to represent or stand for another, is using a sign or a symbol. The stick (an object) stands for a wand; the block of wood stands for a mobile phone; the child stands for the mother. This ability to move beyond the perceived object to an imagined object and to use the concrete object as a sign of the imagined object is very important in cognitive development. As you know we use symbolic systems to communicate (speaking, listening, reading, writing, drawing, music, dance) and to solve problems (numerals, signs) and so on. Success in schooling and in life depends on this ability to go beyond the concrete and into the abstract. This marks the first step on the journey and we call this the *symbolic function*.

Vygotsky says that what happens here is a reversal of the initial response to the investigation of objects where the object dominates the meaning. The meaning now dominates the object. The piece of wood *is* a wand and the world *is* now the world of magic; the building block *is* the mobile phone and the child can begin to communicate with others using it; the child *is* the mother and can play out anything in her experience that pleases or concerns her. Here is how Vygotsky expressed this:

> In a critical moment, when for a child a stick is a horse, i.e. when an object (a stick) constitutes a prop for separating the meaning of a horse from a real horse, the fraction becomes reversed and the sense: sense/object becomes predominant
>
> (1978: 80)

This is important because it marks a significant moment for the child in terms of some of the things we have talked about in earlier chapters. The real object in the play situation enables the child to use a sign as the tool (the real object becomes a sign or symbol for something else) in verbal thinking. If you talk to a very young child about a horse, for example, the child might look around to see if he or she can find one – a search for the horse as object. If you talk to an older child about a horse the child can picture or imagine a horse without having to have a real or a toy one to hand. The child using the stick as a horse is making a detachment of the *meaning* of a horse from a real horse. The child, using the object, is on the way to being able to think abstractly. So the child, using an object in play, moves from needing the object to internalising an image or memory of the object to be able to play at making magic or riding a horse without needing the physical props. You will have seen young children using one thing to stand for another and, as they get older, being able to imagine things as they play. Here are two extremes:

1   Two-year-old Colin uses a mop bucket as a pram and a football as a baby.
2   Four-year-old Parmjit climbs to the top of the climbing tower and starts to crawl across the ladder placed on the top, shouting, 'Look out! The bear is there, coming up the slope. Hide yourself!'

In the first example Colin is using physical objects to represent things. The mop bucket becomes the pram with the ball, as baby, inside. The play he then engages in revolves around pushing the baby in the pram, feeding the baby and talking to the baby. The meaning he has given the objects (turning them into signs or symbols) has taken over from the reality.

Parmjit does not need to have a real bear in her play. She has internalised concepts around bears and danger and shouts to her friends, partaking in her play, to protect themselves from the danger she has imagined.

The concept of meaning

Some of what we are going to look at here is complicated, but understanding it is important to grasping the significance of language and thought. A word does not just apply to one single object. A word concerns a whole group or class of objects. If we look back to the example of a child using a stick to represent a horse, the word horse does not refer to one particular animal but rather to a class or animals – those that are tall, neigh, can be ridden and have four legs, four hoofs and a tail. According to Vygotsky meaning comes about in four phases and involves the child in making *generalisations*. The four phases of generalisation he identified were:

1   syncretic images;
2   complexes;
3   preconcepts; and
4   scientific concepts.

Let us look at these in order.

1   In the first phase, the creation of the *syncretic image*, the child is able to know what bears and horses and lions and elephants are, but may not yet be able to deal with the concept of animals. Understanding that concept requires being able to generalise features from discrete objects in order to group and classify

them in some way. Perhaps the child decides that all creatures with four legs are animals.
2 This leads the child into the second phase, where objects can be lined up and gathered together under one general meaning. *Complexes* thus occur according to features the child has identified as similar in terms of function or purpose between the objects in her discrete groups. So the child might be able to put knives and forks together because she is able to identify that they are both used as eating tools.
3 *Preconcepts* refer to the ability to use symbols in order to represent something, so the child might draw something or write a word for something.
4 *Scientific concepts* are the concepts that children began to be able to construct through formal teaching. Vygotsky believed that concepts could be called scientific where they were conscious.

Here, in Vygotsky's own words, is an example:

> In our experiments, a child who rarely spoke learned the meanings of five words (i.e. chair, table, cabinet, couch, bookcase) with no particular difficulty. He clearly would have been able to extend the series. However, he could not learn the word 'furniture'. Though the child could easily learn any word from the series of subordinate concepts, this more general word was impossible for him. Learning the word 'furniture' represented something more than the addition of a sixth word to the five that the child had already mastered. It represented the mastery of the relationship of generality. The mastery of the word 'furniture' represented the mastery of the child's first higher order concept, a concept that would include a series of more specific subordinate concepts.
>
> (Vygotsky 1987: 225)

You may well be scratching your head by now and asking yourself, 'What does this have to do with play?' Vygotsky suggests that the most highly developed form of complex is the *pseudoconcept*. He suggested that this develops most commonly at around the stage children start engaging in pretend play. So here is our link with play. This is a term we have not yet looked at and it is not mentioned in the phases of becoming able to generalise that we looked at earlier. Read on to learn little more about pseudoconcepts. Vygotsky said that the transition from complexes to concepts is made possible by the use of pseudoconcepts. What he meant was that children need to develop and use pseudoconcepts before they can use concepts. You will know that pseudo- means 'false' and pseudoconcepts seem like concepts that are not fully developed because the bonds between the different elements of the pseudoconcepts are associative or experiential rather than logical and abstract. Remember that concepts mean that the learner no longer has to depend on concrete experience but uses internalised experience to be conscious of what she knows. The learner uses the pseudoconcept in talking or in activities as if it were a true concept. You may have heard a child use a word in conversation with you or another adult and use the word in a way which indicates that although the child uses the word, the meaning of the word is not fully understood:

> Sammy, when very little and wanting to say something would state 'I want to make a proclamation'.

You can see how she knew that a proclamation was something verbal and because she wanted to say something she used the word aptly but not fully understanding its meaning. (You will encounter another use of pseudoconcepts in the example of Conrad in the section that follows.)

To help make the link between pseudoconcepts and play here is an example drawn from the work of Dziurla (n.d.). He calls it 'walking the dog'. If an adult and a child are talking about a dog they clearly understand one another. They know what they are talking about. They might be able to talk about different breeds and their behaviour or about their own dogs or cartoon dogs. What they share in common is the object – the notion of 'dog'. On this they converge. Now the adult talking about 'dog' may well be dealing with an abstract concept of a particular type of animal whereas for the child the word may well call up a picture of a particular barking animal. The child has in mind a set of features – more like a picture than a concept.

Now that same adult comes home late from work and sitting over dinner says to the same child, 'It's a dog's life. I am so tired!' The child may well draw up the same picture he did before but this does not allow him to understand what it is the adult is telling him. His pseudoconceptual complex does not allow him to shift from the concrete to the *metaphoric*, which is what the adult is doing. The adult is capable of using a metaphor – my life is as exhausting as the life of a dog. This requires the ability to compare, which, you know, is a higher mental function. Dziurla argues that the pseudoconcept marks the borderline between the two worlds – that of adults and that of children. This borderline is crossable and there is clearly a border area where adults and children meet. This area concerns real, concrete objects and the border creates mental processes of thinking.

You may well be still scratching your head in bewilderment so let us look at some examples of play and see if they enable us to track this borderline, helping the child move towards higher order thinking and firm concepts.

> Arvind and Amy are playing in the water tray. There are a number of objects in the water – a sponge, two corks (one with a hole in it), some plastic toys, paper (probably unintentionally there) and some metal nuts. An adult GH is observing the children and making notes of their comments as part of the requirement to assess children's learning.
> Amy picks up the cork with a hole in it and drops it in the water.

Amy: Look it's lying on the top
(Arvind throws the sponge in the water.)
Amy: It's also on top of the water.
GH: Yes, they both float. I wonder why.
Amy: 'Cos they've got holes.
GH: That's a good guess. The cork has got a hole in it and the sponge has got little holes, hasn't it?
Arvind: And these.
(He picks up some metal nuts and drops them in the water. They do have holes in them but don't, of course, float.)
Arvind: Hmm. Those dropped to the bottom.

These children are three years old and they have chosen to play in the water, and their play has been somewhat hijacked by the adult who moves from observing them to trying to teach them a concept – that of floating. You can see that neither child uses the new word, and the only example we have of generalising is Amy and Arvind both realising that the cork, the sponge and the metal nuts all have holes. You may choose to analyse this example differently but it seems to me that the adult did not give them enough time to actually explore (in other words to have experiential and concrete exploration of the objects in water) before moving on to getting them to try and take on board the concept of floating.

This incident was observed by a colleague visiting a teaching student and is very similar to one recorded by Pramling and Samuelsson (2001) in an article about children's water play. These researchers used a *Piagetian* framework for their analysis of children's learning in developmental stages, but their finding is interesting to those of us taking a more social view. The teacher, in this case, was working with one child and was interacting with the child by offering verbal support for the development of his scientific concepts. So the teacher repeated any prediction made by him in a questioning tone, suggesting the child needed to think more about what he had predicted. For example at one point the child, when asked what would happen to a cork with no hole in it, said it would float and in response to the teacher's question responded 'Yes, when the water comes in, then it starts to sink'. The teacher questioned his response again, 'Water comes in and so it begins to sink?'

The next example comes from an observation made by Geraldine Lanigan (1998). She was observing children in the early years setting playing with magnets.

Willy (three years, 11 months) picks up two magnets. He begins to push them together and pull them apart. 'Look what it can do!' He continues pulling them apart and watching as they come together again. Damian (four years, three months), who is standing watching picks up the magnets when Willy puts them down. He puts them together and puts them up to his eyes. 'I'm making swimming goggles.' He then stands them together on their poles. 'Look, a bridge!'

Damian now puts the magnets on the table. They attract. He then picks up one of the magnets and a wooden brick. Nothing happens. He tries with the glue pot. Again, nothing happens. 'It won't stick to the brick or the glass, but it sticks to the paper clip.'

I then ask, 'I wonder why?'

Damian tries the sponge and then the metal sharpener. As the sharpener moves across the table towards the magnet Damian begins to laugh. 'That shoots down, look!' He picks up the spoon. 'Yeah, a spoon'll stick and a knife. Both do stick to the magnet. It's a bit of a funny trick.'

I say, 'Some things did stick, but some didn't.'

Damian says, 'Let's put them in a pile.' He begins to put the metal things back on the tray.

Ollie (three years, ten months), who has been watching from across the room comes over. He asks, 'Do hands stick?' He picks up one of the magnets and holds it against the palm of his hand.

Damian responds, 'No.'

'Why?' asks Ollie.

'Because it hasn't got the thing – the magnet thing.'

I repeat his response, 'The magnet thing?'

Damian goes on, 'The bit that sticks.'

Damian and Ollie begin to go around the classroom trying the magnets against the different surfaces – e.g. the wall, the wooden shelves, the books.

Damian says, excitedly, 'It sticks on the radiator.'

The boys return to the table and try the magnet on the surface of the table. Ollie says, 'Not on the table.'

Damian says, 'Magnet them all up.'

He holds the magnet over the table and watches the metal items rise up. He shouts to me, 'Gerardine, look!'

I say, 'Some things are still on the table.'

'They haven't got the right things in them, the right bits and bobs. Look, look!'

The metal sharpener attracts the paper clips. Willy, who has been watching Damian from the book corner, now returns to the table. He tries the wall nut, the glass pot and the knife. He then goes straight to the radiator. He returns to the table and waves the magnet over the paper clips and says, 'Every time I try to take them off they come back on again.'

Willy begins to sort all the things which are attracted to the magnet. He lines them up in a straight row and puts all the remaining objects back on the tray. He then stands one of the magnets on its pole. The metal items move towards the magnet. He says, 'It's a river going under a bridge.'

Meanwhile Emma (four years, seven months) picks up the other magnet and waves it over the table. She giggles as it collects the paper clips.

> I say, 'I wonder why they stick.'
> Emma points to the poles and says, 'This bit.'
> I ask, 'What's so special about that bit?'
> She replies, 'Well, it sticks and it's a magnet bit. I'm going to try something magic. I'm going to try to get these bits off if I can.'
>
> (Lanigan 1998: 35–6)

This is a wonderful account of children at play, interacting with one another and with an adult and moving clearly through naming individual items and generalising through hands-on experience to identify those that are attracted and those that are repelled. The adult in this case interacts but makes no real attempt to teach the children anything. Rather she directs their attention to specific features like the poles on the magnets. You will notice that the children, at play, are revealing just how much they know and how busy they are as problem solvers.

And this, perhaps, brings us to the heart of the matter. But one more example before we reveal this. This is taken from the work of Susan Isaacs and refers to what she calls *make-believe* and *hypothesis*. Susan Isaacs was working with children in the 1920s, when she set up the Maltings House School in Cambridge. She was deeply concerned about some of the theories about young children and their learning so she set about letting the children take the lead whilst she observed, recorded and responded to them. Her book *Intellectual Growth in Young Children* was first published in 1930 and is full of her perceptive observation notes and her analysis of what these told her about the children, their interests, and their learning and development. Here she tells us of Phineas, aged only three years and ten months, when, through pretend play, you see him making the first steps to rescue meaning from the here and now of a concrete situation to enable him to become conscious of his own ability to behave 'as if' and to hypothesise:

> Phineas and some other children had made a ship in the classroom, using table and chairs. Phineas played a largely passive role as a passenger on the ship and was busy stitching a canvas bag. One of the adults was with them on the ship. The other children were playing a range of roles. Then Phineas ran out of thread and the adult suggested he get it out of the drawer. Phineas, totally in role, said 'I can't get out of the ship while it's going, can I?' and called out to the captain 'Stop the ship! I want to get out!' The captain eventually agreed and the ship was brought to a 'landing stage' and Phineas got out, fetched the thread, got on again and stated 'Now you can go on again'.
>
> (Isaacs 1930: 105)

Phineas, engaged in pretend play, revealed his very complex abilities to behave *as if* he were on a ship, although he had never been on one. More than that he showed that could *hypothesise* what would happen if he tried to get off a moving ship – again, although he had never been on one. So, through his play, he was able to bring together not only his own experiences and memories, but all the concepts he had built relating to this notion of 'being on a ship'. He knows that a person could not get off a moving ship at sea in order to go and fetch thread from a drawer in the classroom. And this is a child who is not yet four years old. It marks a remarkable feat of thinking.

In another observation Isaacs tells us about two five-year-olds examining two or three holes in the trunk of an apple tree, partly filled with leaf mould.

> They brought water and poured it into one hole, and were very amused when it came out of another lower down. Dan looking at a hole higher up than the one they poured the water into, said 'Perhaps it'll come out of this one'. Miss D. asked, 'Do you think that's possible?' Conrad replied 'No, not unless there's pressure behind it.'
>
> (Isaacs 1930: 112–13)

Isaacs in her analysis of this notes that it is unlikely that Conrad understood the full meaning of what he had said or that he had a clear abstract understanding of the word pressure. For him it was a pseudoconcept. Her explanation is interesting:

> What is most probable is that at some recent date the children had been discussing some questions of how the water got into the bathroom taps (they were always asking that sort of question) and had had the explanation that it came out of the taps on a high floor, in spite of the fact that water does not run uphill, because there was pressure behind it. And then Conrad applied it to the new situation of the holes in the tree. This by no means makes it purely verbal because holes in a tree are very different from brass taps in a bathroom. There must have been some appreciation of the common element – how and when will water come out of a higher hole than it is put in?
>
> (Isaacs 1930: 81)

Play with rules

Here is another definition to add to our list.

Definition 7   In pretend play children develop rules and often these relate to making one thing stand for another. This allows the child to use the symbol or sign so created to move beyond the object or person, to the meaning the child assigns that object or person. This is the first step on the road to higher mental functioning.

In order to survive in the social world all children have to learn the rules that apply to their own families, communities and cultures. In some cultures it is regarded as rude to look an adult in the eyes; in others it is regarded as polite to ask to 'get down' from the table after dinner. Children learn these through their interactions with significant others as they move from babyhood to early childhood and beyond. We have said that any imaginary situation contains rules of behaviour invented by the child or negotiated by children. When the child imagines herself as a sister she has to apply the rules she believes that apply to being a sister. Vygotsky, in his 1933 paper, *Play and its Role in the Mental Development of the Child* (published in English in 1967), described a remarkable observation carried out by a colleague, Sully, where two sisters, aged five and seven, decided to play at being sisters: they were making the play situation and reality come together. What is important about this is that in life the child just is a sister and does not have to think about what being a sister means. In play, being a sister has to be consciously constructed and Vygotsky suggests that the rule created is:

> I must always be a sister in relation to that other sister throughout our play.

Every action taken by the sisters in this play event must then conform to this rule. When the game is over the child, having conformed to the rules in play, internalises them and possibly conforms to them. It is clear that for Vygotsky, children learn the rules of behaviour appropriate to their contexts and cultures through pretend play.

Children move on from playing with objects to playing at 'being others', and it is evident that this play allows them to appropriate or take on the sociocultural practices they are familiar with. The earliest role play often involves children in acting out the most familiar of all roles – mother, father, sister, brother, grandpa and so on. This play later extends to trying out the roles in the mesosystem (where home and local facilities in the life of the child meet), where the child begins to interact with and think about the roles of people like the nurse, the doctor, the postman, the shopkeeper, the teachers and so on. Each of the roles children try out involves working out a complex network of standards of conduct and conventional expectations. Here are two children playing school at home. Wahida is ten years old and Sayeda is eight years old. Wahida as the teacher has a small blackboard and Sayeda, the pupil, has a notebook.

Wahida: What's 24 times four? If you can't do it, there's another easier way to do times. We do lattice. Yes, Sayeda? Good girl for putting your hand up.
Sayeda: I can't do lattice.
Wahida: OK. We'll do one together. OK? We'll do 24 times four. First we draw a box … Then we do two lines that way, the diagonal way. Yes … well done.
[…]
Wahida: The first sum is 30 times five equals … If you want to do lattice you

can. Or you can do your own way, or you can do in your mind, but I would love to see some working out.

(Williams 2004: 62)

Wahida knows how to be the teacher. She knows the tone of voice, the intonation patterns and the particular phrases to use and has also internalised the concept of the importance of giving praise. Just listen to the voice of the teacher you can hear through her comments like 'Good girl for putting your hand up' or 'well done'. Throughout this and the other examples given in Williams' wonderful chapter, Wahida, when in the role of teacher, stays within the rules of being teacher that she has worked out and appropriated. You may have seen a video clip made many years ago by the Open University. It shows four-year-old Helen playing the role of canteen manager. She may never have seen a canteen manager but she has encountered people who are in charge and who organise things so that they work efficiently. Her voice, her mannerisms and the language she uses throughout the clip are those of a manager. All of this is, of course, playful, but it is also serious in that the child, through observation and interaction, posits some rules. She then acts them out in the safety of play and in doing that becomes conscious of the rules. She has to be conscious of them in order to abide by them in the play.

Vygotsky believed that there was no such thing as play without rules. In play, taking on the rules of being someone else is what gives the child pleasure and satisfaction. He also believed that pretend play was, at first, a precursor to creativity. So creativity and imagination are actually formed through play itself. He said,

Play is more nearly recollection of something that has actually happened than imagination. It is more memory in action than a novel imaginary situation.

(1978: 103)

You will know that in later childhood, as children start school, it is games with rules that begin to dominate much of the play. Now rules begin to predominate but it seems that there is always some element of the pretend and some implied imaginary situation related to the game and its rules. It is as though role play becomes rule play and this may mark the development from a reliance on contextual supports (which are offered within the roles children choose to play, which in themselves define the rules) to cognitive abstractions in the form of internalised rules. And all of this, of course, takes place through initial social-contextual processes. And here is the last of our definitions:

Definition 8   Play then moves from role play, where children appropriate the rules of the roles they choose, to play games where the rules dominate but pretend is still possible. Play is memory in action.

Revising your views of play

This has been a chapter with many familiar and unfamiliar ideas. Those of you reading this book will already know much about play, particularly about why you offer children opportunities to play throughout your class and setting. For some of you there will be a concern that play opportunities decrease due to the increase in demands for earlier and earlier meeting of targets. The new Early Years Foundation Stage is already requiring you to ensure that children learn formally far earlier than they do in any other country in the world; with your growing understanding of the importance of first-hand everyday experience, which allows children to build on what they know in situations which make human sense to them, this will be of grave concern. Learning more about why researchers and theorists believe that play – particularly symbolic and pretend play – is important not only for children's social and emotional development but also for their cognitive development will, we hope, make you ensure that you continue to offer children many opportunities to follow their own passions and interests as they interact with others, use cultural tools and solve problems.

Looking back, looking ahead

Vygotsky talked about the following:

1 Play with objects, and its importance in helping children begin the journey to being able to think abstractly. They do this through the *decontextualisation* of meaning – being able to make one thing stand for or represent another.
2 Play in which children are able to adopt roles and make and change rules, which Vygotsky saw as the *appropriation* of sociocultural practices. The children play the roles they intentionally choose to play and invent the rules that explain and structure their play to their satisfaction.
3 Play which allows the child to create the zone of proximal development. Vygotsky said, 'In play a child is always above his average age, above his daily behaviour; in play it is as though he were a head taller than himself' (Vygotsky 1967: 16).

We have spent some time looking at play in this chapter, attempting to reach a wide and comprehensive definition of the term in order that we can talk about it with shared understanding. In summary, here are our eight definitions:

1 Play is self-chosen and allows the child to follow her own agenda in order to address her needs or interests. So when a child chooses to play in the home corner and chooses what to do within that play, what we see is real play. When the child goes into the home corner because it is her turn or because someone has told her to, this is not play.
2 It is risk-free in the sense that if things don't go according to plan the plan

can change since the child is in charge. So there is no possibility of failure.
3   Because the child has chosen to play the play itself is deeply engaging and involving and can last for a few seconds or over days or even weeks. It can be solitary or involve others. Often, but not always, it involves an imaginary world in which signs and symbols may play a part.
4   Although play may be solitary it is almost certainly social in origin in that the child will often play out things they have experienced with others. Interaction with others is often, although not always, part of play.
5   Play is mediated by cultural tools such as signs and symbols, and (we will return to this) toys and other objects, and, of course, by language.
6   In play children, since they control the play, can express, in safety, their fears, anger, joy, jealousy or other feelings. So there is an affective element to play.
7   In pretend play children develop rules and often these relate to making one thing stand for another. This allows the child to use the symbol or sign so created to move beyond the object or person, to the meaning the child assigns that object or person. This is the first step on the road to higher mental functioning.
8   Play then moves from role play, where children appropriate the rules of the roles they choose, to play games where the rules dominate but pretend is still possible. Play is memory in action.

From this it has emerged that play is an extremely complex and fascinating phenomenon, and not something that can easily be dismissed as being fun. Rather, it is a serious business involving children in taking steps to move from dependence to independence. Be careful of using catchphrases like 'play is children's work' without clearly understanding just what it is that is significant and serious about play.

In the next chapter we sidestep slightly, returning to the idea of scaffolding and considering in more depth how you can use it to help the learners in your care. The diagram below illustrates the gap between the performance and the potential level, and shows that in the gap – in the zone of proximal development – children are assisted to move beyond what they have shown they can do in everyday activities by having their learning scaffolded, using cultural tools, playing 'as if' they were someone or something else and in doing that adopting roles to match the rules they have generated. Figure 7.1 is intended to help you see the links between some of the things we have been talking about.

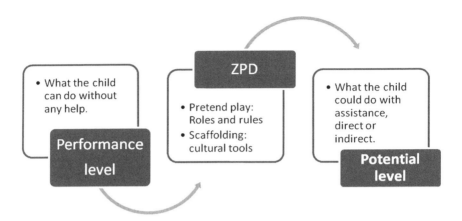

Figure 7.1 Assisting a child through the zone of proximal development

Glossary

Word or phrase	What it means	Why it is significant
appropriation of sociocultural practice	To take on board the ideas or practices of a group.	Another important idea in regard to how children move from being on the periphery of a community of practice to being at its heart.
complexes	The ability to hold wider ideas of things through identifying significant features – for example, furniture.	Further on the way to higher order thinking
decontextualisation of meaning	The developing ability to think about something when it is not present.	Essential to understand this because it is the key to why play is so important as a way of learning, particularly in the early years.

free-flow play	Another of Bruce's terms, this time to describe play that is self-chosen and in which children become deeply involved.	
generalisation	To move from the particular to the general.	Higher order concept.
hypothesise	To come up with a theory about what might happen if…	Higher order concept.
make-believe	Synonymous with pretend – the ability to act 'as if' or think about 'what if'.	
play as an integrating mechanism	Tina Bruce's view that it is in play that children are able to bring together all they have learned	This is an interesting view, particularly if you think of it in terms of the ZPD.
play as preparation for life	A while ago some theorists believed that children played in order to prepare themselves for being adults. This is a rather diminished view and one which sees childhood as preparation for adulthood.	You decide if this is how you would like to see play.
preconcepts	The ability to use symbols to represent something.	Higher order concept.
pseudoconcepts	Assists the transition from concepts to abstract thinking; often indicated by a child using a word without fully understanding its meaning.	

symbolic function	A very important step on the road to abstract thinking, this is the ability to make one thing represent another and marks the beginning of the decontextualisation of meaning.	On the way to higher order thinking and very important in understanding why play is so important in learning.
syncretic images	The ability to hold discrete images of things – for example, chair and table.	On the way to higher order thinking.

Chapter 8

On bridging the gap
More about the ZPD

In this chapter we turn our attention to looking at what actually happens when the child is enabled to move beyond the level she displays in the classroom or setting to a higher level of functioning. We will discuss a number of strategies or techniques and these include the following:

- scaffolding;
- sustained shared thinking;
- guided participation;
- ownership and appropriation;
- reciprocal or peer teaching – becoming the more expert other;
- questioning and theories;
- feedback.

Scaffolding

The term scaffolding was used by Jerome Bruner (1997b) as a response to his reading of Vygotsky's work on the zone of proximal development. He borrowed the term from the construction industry where, as you will know, a scaffold is a temporary support erected to allow the building of a tall structure to be completed successfully (or repaired or painted successfully). On completion the scaffold is removed. So Bruner borrowed the word to explain the interactional support, often in the form of adult–child dialogue, that is structured by the adult to maximise the growth of the child's *intrapsychological* (which means what happens inside the learner) functioning (Clay and Cazden, 1990). The support or scaffold is gradual and is only withdrawn when the child has achieved mastery of the task. Bruner's account of what the teacher or more experienced learner must do in order to scaffold learning is interesting and is summarised here.

The teacher must:

1. *protect* the learner from distraction by highlighting the significant feature or features of the problem;

2 *sequence* the steps to enable understanding;
3 *enable negotiation* between teacher and learner;
4 *know* just what it is that the learner needs in order to succeed.

This last point is important, suggests Bruner, because it raises the issue of how culture gets internalised by the mediation of others. Drawing on the work of Tomasello *et al.* (1993), Bruner suggests that successful *transmission* of culture requires features such as a tutor who shares the child's culture, or some shared agreement about how the teacher and learner will operate within the school or setting. The message from this is clear: learners are more likely to reach their potential when they are supported by those with whom they share cultural tools – e.g. language.

Datta, in her book *Bilinguality and Literacy* (2000), gives several examples of how the learning of young bilingual children is supported by either having access to someone who shares their language or to physical and visible tools to build shared meaning. She cites the example of a teacher working with a five-year-old bilingual girl, Seema. The children in the class had been involved in a mathematical activity, which involved them in making boxes. When, at the end of the session, Seema was invited to show her work to the rest of the class she couldn't, because she didn't understand what was required. Then the support worker, understanding her problem, used more careful language with the child to help her and also pointed to the box that the child had made. This made it possible for Seema to show her box to the others, and when the teacher asked her 'How did you make it?' the support worker, again understanding Seema's dilemma, held up a pair of scissors. This enabled Seema, in turn, to point to the pair of scissors and so show what she had learned. So Seema, who might have been seen as having failed to complete the task, was, in fact, able to demonstrate both the end product and the process.

Here is another example of Seema in class, this time having her learning scaffolded as she reads a book with her teacher and her friend Anya. They were reading a version of *Little Red Hen* which they had heard read in class story session and they had also sat and looked at it together on many occasions. As they came to the refrain 'And who will help me?' the two little girls joined in with the teacher. Anya was more confident than Seema, who appeared to just move her lips. Afterwards Seema chose to 'read' the book to the teacher and turned pages until she got to a familiar picture and the refrain she knew. She read this and then turned the page and read the refrain again. The teacher, recognising her struggle, pointed to the adjacent page on which was written '"Not I" said the cat'. Seema looked at the teacher but said nothing. The adult read the text and this time Seema looked down at the text on the page. This one-to-one scaffolding shows how a sensitive teacher can successfully intervene to take the child to the next step, however small, without destroying the child's confidence.

If you have ever led or participated in a *shared reading activity* using a *large format book* you will almost certainly have either been involved in or witnessed scaffolding in action. Here is an example from my own personal observation for you to consider. As you do, think about the four points raised earlier – namely, protecting the learner from distraction by highlighting the significant feature or features of the problem; sequencing the steps to enable understanding; enabling negotiation between teacher and learner; and knowing just what it is that the learner needs in order to succeed.

Alison is the teacher in the reception class. Many of her children are speakers of other languages and she tries to ensure that for her shared reading/writing sessions she has access to a support worker who speaks one of the major languages. She is trying to introduce all the children to rhymes and has asked some of them to bring in rhymes their mums and dads know and a few parents have helped so she has a couple of Bengali rhymes and one Greek rhyme. Today she is using a large format nursery rhyme book which gives her a template for the nursery rhyme she, and the children, are jointly going to chant and write. Today's rhyme is 'The Grand Old Duke of York'. She chose it because the children will not have to compose anything: the rhyme already exists. They can concentrate solely on the transcriptional skills of writing. She also chose it because she knows the children enjoy doing the actions of 'up' and 'down' (or 'half way up' and 'half way down'). She knows what they already know and her intention is to draw their attention to how the repetition in the rhyme, which she makes easily visible on the page, can make the reading of the rhyme easier.

The children sit on the carpet around her with the support worker seated close to the Sylheti/Bengali speakers. She has a note pad on an easel and is going to use a large pen to demonstrate the writing. But they start by chanting the Bengali rhyme they learned yesterday and she is pleased to see all the children joining in and doing the actions. Then she asks how many know the new rhyme and about half the children put up their hands. Alison then invites them all to join her in saying the rhyme and doing the actions. She starts slowly and speeds up and as she does so the children become more animated and join in with gusto. Throughout the whole activity she keeps the attention of the children and protects them from distraction. She then starts by writing 'The Grand Old Duke of York' at the top of the page and reminds the children this is the title. She then asks a child who she knows will know the answer where she should put her pen in order to start writing. The child comes up and points to the left-hand side of the page, underneath the title. She starts to write.

Oh, the grand old duke of …

and then stops and says to them, 'I know that the word "York" is already on this page. Who can find it?' When Julio finds it she praises him lavishly and when she gets to the end of the line she moves her pen to the line below to align the text. So we have

> Oh, the grand old duke of York
> He had ten thousand men

Alison then stops and asks the child, 'What do you notice about the words ten and men?' Mara shouts out, 'They rhyme! They rhyme! You told us yesterday.'

'Great, Mara,' says Alison. 'You remembered!' She involves the children in helping her know where to start each new line, sometimes how to write the first letter of a word and sometimes to suggest what might come next. By now we have

> Oh, the grand old duke of York
> He had ten thousand men
> He marched them up to the top of the hill
> And he marched them down again
> And when they were up,
> they were up
> And when they were down,
> they were down

Alison then invites Julio to have a go at writing 'And when they were …' on the next line. She chooses him because he is keen and likely to succeed. More than that he has a model to use in the text on the page. When he has completed this, with some help, she finishes the rhyme off and they all read it aloud. At the end she asks some of the children to come up and point to any of the words that they recognise or can read, or words which start with the same letter as their own name (Personal observation).

It is easy to identify points at which Alison scaffolds the children's learning. She starts with what they already know and enjoy (nursery rhymes). She doesn't coerce them into doing anything, but *selects particular pupils* to act as *role models or peer teachers*. She *sequences* the steps, *manages negotiation* and *gives feedback* when she *praises appropriately and in detail* as when she praises Mara for remembering. You will almost certainly be able to come up with other examples of adults scaffolding the learning of young children in formal settings.

Sustained shared thinking

This is a term you are almost certain to have heard of. It is the current 'buzz' word to discuss the learning and teaching of children in the early years and it arises largely from the findings of the Researching Effective Pedagogy in the Early Years (REPEY) project. In trying to identify 'good practice' in a range of settings (fourteen in number) the researchers looked at four aspects: the interactions between children and adults; aspects of the curriculum; links with home and community; and issues around behaviour. We will limit our discussion to the first of these. In the settings which were rated most highly by the previous and larger Effective Provision for Pre-School Education (EPPE) project they found, and this will certainly not surprise you, that the most important factor was the quality of adult–child interactions. These were the settings where children, as a consequence, made the most progress and where the activities were founded on solid principles of direct and first-hand experience where children were able and helped to construct new understandings. In the views of the researchers, what characterised the quality they identified was the evidence of opportunities for children to become deeply involved in meaningful activities together with adults, both sharing meaning and engaged with understanding one another. They noted that the learning that took place through these interventions was particular in what they called *sustained shared thinking* between a pair (or a *dyad*) of learner and adult. In their views this notion adds to the concept of scaffolding and can be identified as an activity characterised by three key points:

1   The adult both pays attention to what the child is doing or wanting to do, and has sufficient knowledge of her own in terms of the subject or activity involved.

This is essential if the teacher is to respond appropriately to the child. I would emphasise that specialist knowledge in the early years is more likely to be about how children learn best and not about any particular subject. With older children, as they come to explore and understand abstract concepts, it is clear that the adults involved with the child do need knowledge and understanding of what it is the child is learning.

2   The child is aware of what is to be learned or what is in an adult's mind or 'required' by the activity.

In schools there is a tendency to put the learning outcomes up on the board at the beginning of a session. It is a good idea to help children know what it is you are hoping they will learn, but younger children will learn what interests and concerns them and although you may have learning outcomes for them these may not be shared. How they can become shared is through the comments you make or the questions you ask. Do you remember Helen who was such an effective canteen manager (see page 115)? At one point when she was being observed Helen approached an adult with a toy frying pan in which were some blocks. 'Sausages,' she announced, as she showed the pan to the adult. 'Oh,' said the adult, 'how many have you got?' With a withering look Helen walked off. The adult had imposed a learning outcome unrelated to what the child had been doing and this revealed the adult's insensitivity and inability to tune in to the child's agenda.

3   There is active co-construction of an idea or a skill.

By co-construction they mean that the adult and child together do this.

Read the case study below to see this in action. We see an adult with a group of nursery age children who are sitting at a table playing with play dough. The adult, a nursery nurse, is referred to as NNEB 1 and the child, aged three years eleven months, as Boy 1. (Note: my comments are in square brackets and italics.)

Boy 1:   (Hands her a ball of play dough.)
NNEB 1: I wonder what is inside? I'll unwrap it.
[*The adult feeds the child an idea.*]
NNEB 1: (Quickly makes the ball into a thumb pot and holds it out to BOY 1.)
It's empty.
Boy 1:   (Takes a pinch of play dough and drops into a thumb pot.)
It's an egg.
NNEB 1: (Picking it out gingerly.)
It's a strange shape.
(Another child tried to take the 'egg'.)
(To Boy 1) What's it going to hatch into?
Boy 1:   A lion.
NNEB 1: A lion?… Oh I can see why it might hatch into a lion, it's got little hairy bits on it.
[*The adult takes the child's idea seriously.*]
(NNEB 1 sends Boy 1 to put the egg somewhere safe to hatch. He takes the egg and goes into the bathroom. After a few minutes BOY 1 returns to the group.)
NNEB 1: Has the egg hatched?
[*The adult shows that she has remembered what it was the child was exploring.*]
Boy 1:   Yes.
NNEB 1: What was it?
Boy 1:   A bird.
NNEB 1: A bird. We'll have to take it outside at playtime and put it in a tree so it can fly away.
(Siraj-Blatchford *et al.*, 2002: Document 421, Vignette 8)

Guided participation

This term was used by Barbara Rogoff (1990), who looked at the learning that took place through everyday activities in the lives of children in a range of countries, some of them developing countries. She saw children being *apprentices in thinking* to the adults and to more expert others within their communities. This links back to sustained shared thinking in that the research refers back to the work of researchers like Wells (1985) and Bruner (1966) who had looked at how children acquire their first language. To do that they had looked at children and their carers engaged in everyday activities within the home and noted that child and adult had to have a sharing of meaning in order for communication to take place and meaning to be constructed. Here is an example to illustrate this:

> 14-month-old Malika crawled over to her toy box and took out every toy. She then looked at her mother and started to cry. 'What is it you want?' asked her mother, going over to the box to see if she could identify what it was the baby could clearly not find. She saw the arm of a doll sticking out from underneath the rug and held it up. 'Is this it?' A big smile was both the answer to her question and a reward for her perseverance.

A very easy to analyse and everyday occurrence. Parents and carers and educators of very young children have to find ways of guessing what it is the child wants or is doing or is trying to find out in order to meet her needs. For learning to take place this sharing of meaning and purpose has to be in place. We have talked in earlier chapters about the importance of words as cultural tools and have seen how language can mediate learning. Here we have to introduce a new term and a new concept – that of *intersubjectivity*. We use the word to mean the shared meanings that people construct through their interactions with one another as they use cultural tools to interpret the meanings of their social or cultural or intellectual lives. The point of raising it here is that intersubjectivity emphasises that shared cognition or thinking and agreement are essential ingredients in learning. Vygotsky (1987) himself says that intersubjectivity provides the bridge between the known and the new. Think about that in terms of learning. If we are to bridge the gap between the actual and possible, the performance and the potential levels, we move the child from the known to the new. Intersubjectivity provides the basis for communication and points to the possible extension of the child's understanding. For Rogoff there are lessons to be learned from the models of adults and children who are alongside one another in the everyday tasks of planting, cooking, weaving, selling or other work in the home or beyond. The tasks themselves, intimately rooted in the needs and the lives of the people, allow for meaning to be shared. Children have models to observe and words to listen to as they first watch and then participate in the life of their community. In this way they are drawn from the periphery into the centre, as full members of a community of practice.

Clare Kelly (2004) explains how Jamie, in the nursery, came to literacy through his passion for technology, particularly for Buzz Lightyear. He came, too, with a rich fund of knowledge about what he had seen and discussed with his two principal carers, his mum and his grandma. The staff at the nursery noticed how characters from popular culture occurred in all his drawings and model-making and discussion. For example they noted that, as he folded paper to make an aeroplane, he told a member of staff that his nanny had shown him how to do it. The staff did not dismiss his home learning, but saw it as the beginnings of literacy. They chose to recognise and build on the learning that had taken place at home through guided participation. They saw that what they described as his nonchalant attitude to books as opposed to videos or films or television came about because he brought with him, from home, certain expectations about texts and rules for participating in literacy events – which for him involved being with other people watching a screen with moving images on it in the company of people who loved him.

Ownership and appropriation

You will remember that both Bakhtin and Vygotsky saw that children's consciousness – their awareness of their world and those in it – exists only as part of the social and cultural worlds. It is others who induct children into the signs and symbols that are used by both children and adults to interact with and enquire about the world. As children and adults continue to explore this, with the gaps between their understandings growing smaller as meanings are negotiated, children become more and more members of a community of sign-users. In other words it is through interactions with others in meaningful and relevant contexts that children become part of the world of reading, writing, mathematics, art, music and other symbolic systems. Vygotsky reminds us that children '*grow into the intellectual life of those around them*' (1978: 88). In order for children to be able to become full members of their communities they need to be able to appropriate or take ownership of aspects of their lives and worlds.

Two words that occur over and over again when thinking about learning are involvement and engagement. These words are used to indicate that, for this gap to be bridged, the child or learner must be motivated and this implies that the child must feel some sense of ownership of the activity or problem concerned. The very word *appropriation* suggests that the child must take into herself whatever it is that she is interested in and this should become part of herself. This can only happen if and when what the child is involved in matters to the child and matters enough for the child to get so deeply involved in what she is doing that she wants to continue working at it. Lillian Katz has written widely about early years education, and argues (1998) that many of the things that children are asked to do and expected to get involved in are extremely dreary or trivial and certainly not relevant to their needs and interests. She suggests one really has to question how a child can take ownership of such tasks or learn from them. Draw your own conclusions from reading this selection of tasks – all drawn from current classrooms:

Colour all the BIG balloons red and all the SMALL balloons green.

Draw 5 things that start with **r**.

> Sort the shapes [a collection of 2-dimensional squares, rectangles, circles and triangles] into sets.
>
> Copy this sentence on the line below:
> The cat is black.
>
> Children have to learn to chant the names of the months of the year.
>
> Children have to make Christmas cards in a class where only one of the children is Christian.

When adults were questioned as to why these tasks had been given to the children responses ranged from 'They must learn their colours' to 'Because they are educational'. You might well wonder how asking children to do things like that even begins to bridge the gap between what they show they can do and what they might do given the chance to really care about what they are doing.

Reciprocal and peer teaching: becoming the more expert other

In his thinking about the social nature of learning and the role of *more expert others* Vygotsky did not specify that the more expert other should be an adult. For him another child – but one who was more expert than the target child in a particular area – could support the child in bridging the gap. Peer teaching or reciprocal teaching is an interesting outcome of this thinking and much excellent work has been done on this with very young children as well as with older children.

Let us start by taking an example of peer teaching from the work of Kenner. You will remember that, in an earlier chapter, we looked at Ming teaching Amina how to write the Chinese character for the number 7. To remind you here it is again (in a more complete version) and as you read it through ask yourself these questions: What is Ming, who is the more expert other, learning from teaching Amina? What does Amina learn from having Ming scaffold her learning?

> Chinese writing consists of thousands of characters, each of which represents a different meaning. The characters are built up from a repertoire of basic stroke types and stroke patterns. At Chinese school Ming learned to write each stroke with precision in a particular sequence, to produce a correctly rendered character which could not be confused with any similar-looking one. Considerable importance was also placed on the aesthetic value of the final product. In the first-year class there was plenty of discussion between teacher and children about the length and angle of each stroke and its balance with respect to other strokes.
>
> As Ming taught Amina, he put these principles into operation. He

demonstrated the character for 'seven' and Amina tried to follow his model ... At times her version began to look like the English numeral '4'. Ming realized that Amina was likely to interpret Chinese writing from an English point of view; a few moments earlier she had written one of the curved Chinese strokes as if it was the English number '2' and he had commented, 'No, not 2, do it in Chinese.' In this case he told her 'That's a 4 – that's wrong.' At another point Amina's writing resembled the English letter 't' and again Ming noticed this: 'That's wrong – that's a T.' When showing her for the second time he made an aesthetic evaluation of his own work, saying 'That's too lumpy.'

Amina's response was to make more effort to write the character for 'seven' according to the model provided by her 'teacher'. When she went on to learn the character for 'three' she showed that she was beginning to self-critique the details of her Chinese writing.

(Kenner 2004b: 108)

Each time I read through this extract I am struck by how much this six-year-old boy, Ming, knows about the features of two of his sets of cultural tools – the written forms of Chinese and of English. He has developed *metalinguistic knowledge* (which means knowledge about language itself) and he has done this through coming to understand both systems through his interactions with more expert others in his Chinese and his English schools. When put in the role of more expert other with Amina he not only displays what he knows about the subject but also reveals an understanding of why Amina, as a learner, is struggling,. He recognises that she is trying to learn about Chinese characters through generalising from her experience of English numbers, which, to her eye, look similar. He has developed an understanding of the reality that other people have ideas and thoughts and feelings and is able to try and work out what these might be. This is sometimes called *'theory of mind'* – the cognitive ability to attribute desires, needs, thoughts and feelings to others. For me this is a superb example of peer teaching and how both partners in the dyad benefit.

Let us now look at an example of reciprocal teaching. This requires more overt and explicit teaching but it requires a lot of turn taking with the learner and the teacher each taking responsibility for a 'turn' in the learning process. Here is an example:

> Six-year-old Cass wants to know how to work out the concept 'goes into'. Her sister, whilst they were playing school, told her to learn this and so she has asked her teacher. The teacher says, 'Let's start with some blocks to help us. Go and get some for me.'
>
> Cass brings back some of the counting blocks in her classroom.
>
> 'OK,' says the teacher. 'If I ask you to get twenty five blocks and share them out between five people, could you do that?'
>
> Cass counts out 25 blocks and then, using one block at a time, counts 'one

for you, one for you, one for you, one for you and one for you' five times over.

'OK,' says the teacher. 'Tell me what you did.'

'I gave one to each person and then another one and then another one and then another one till they had all gone.'

'Good,' says the teacher. 'You shared them out. How many did each person get?'

Cass counts each pile and says, 'Five.'

'So you worked out that 5 goes 5 times into 25. Now try 27 blocks.'

Cass goes through the whole procedure again and then finds she has two left over. 'What do I do with these?' she asks.

'Good question,' replies the teacher. 'What you have discovered is that 5 goes 5 times into 27 but not exactly. You have got 2 blocks left over.'

(Personal observation)

In this example the more expert other is a teacher but it could equally well be a child. You can see how the teacher, in this example, takes seriously the child's request to learn something and through passing comments back and forth, helps the child internalise what she is learning. The teacher provides her with the language she needs to develop the concept of 'goes into' or 'division' and also allows her to begin to *reflect* on what she is doing as she learns. The teacher, in this reciprocal exchange, is helping the child develop *metacognitive skills* – the ability to reflect on what she has learned.

Questioning and theories

My parents used to tell me the story of what happened when I was a very small child and they took me for a walk to the docks in the seaside town in which we lived in South Africa. There I encountered a metal 'lump' on the ground – the things that the boats were tied up to. My mother said, 'You walked around and touched it and looked at it and smelled it and then you announced, "I seed it and I feeled it and it's not a dog".' With this simple statement I explained very clearly what I had done in order to work out what this familiar object was. I used my senses: I looked and smelled and touched the object and then walked around it. Having done this I then compared it with ideas of things I had in my head that resembled the object in some way. This allowed me to come to the conclusion that it was not a dog. At the age of two I was able to use higher level functions of internalised concepts (the memory of dogs) and comparison. This gave me the beginning of a *theory*. And all of that took place through encountering something unfamiliar and interesting in the company of people with whom I could interact. I can imagine you raising your eyebrows at the thought that very young children can have theories but if you listen to children carefully and analyse what you hear you will realise that this is so. But we need a definition of theory and Rinaldi (2006) has one that I find useful. She says that all of us, on encountering something new or unfamiliar, try to interpret what it is or what it does and we come up with an '*interpretive theory*', which is an explanation that gives meaning to the things and events of the world. For her a theory is something that can be regarded as satisfactory in the sense that the person who arrives at it finds that it answers a question – even though this answer may change with more experience.

In many of the vignettes in this book you will find children asking questions as they play or work alongside others, or listen to stories, or talk to their friends and family, or eat their dinner. You will find children making statements which are in fact tentative or transitory theories. In situations where children are treated equally in the sense of being regarded as equal partners in any social exchange they will feel that they have the right to ask questions and get their questions answered. In many schools and settings, however, teachers are seen to be the ones who ask the questions and children the ones who answer them. But, to return to a much earlier theme in this book, when children explore their world, trying to make sense of it through their movements and their senses before they have access to words, it seems to observers that their behaviour indicates that they are, in fact, and without words, asking first, 'What is this thing? What does it do? What is it for?' And later, when they start to separate the meaning from the object through the beginnings of pretend play, they ask, 'What can I do with this thing? What can I make it become? What will I be when I use this thing?'

To illustrate this we return to an example drawn, yet again, from Isaacs (1930). She charts in her diary what happened when the pet rabbit died.

14.7.25
The rabbit had died in the night. Dan found it and said, 'It's dead – its tummy does not move up and down now.' Paul said, 'My daddy says that if we put it into water, it will get alive again.' Mrs I said, 'Shall we do so and see?' They put it into a bath of water. Some of them said, 'It is alive.' Duncan said, 'If it floats it's dead and if it sinks, it's alive.' It floated on the surface. One of them said, 'It's alive, because it's moving.' This was a circular movement, due to the currents in the water. Mrs I therefore put in a small stick which also moved round and round and they agreed that the stick was not alive. They then suggested that they should bury the rabbit, and all helped to dig a hole and bury it.

Later on, seeing the puppy lying on the grass in the sun, Duncan called out for fun, 'Oh, the puppy's dead!' All the children went to see it, and laughed heartily when the puppy got up and ran at them.

15.7.25
Frank and Duncan talked of digging the rabbit up – but Frank said, 'It's not there – it's gone up to the sky.' They began to dig, but tired of it and ran off to something else. Later they came back and dug again. Duncan, however, said, 'Don't bother – it's gone – it's up in the sky' and gave up digging. Mrs I therefore said 'Shall we see if it's there?' and also dug. They found the rabbit

and were very interested to see it still there. Duncan said 'Shall we cut its head off?' They reburied it.

(Isaacs 1930: 82-3)

This gives a fascinating insight into children's preoccupations and theories. I love their theory of dead things floating and how Susan Isaacs got them to question their theory about dead things not being able to move by putting something they know is not alive – a stick – into the water and seeing that despite not being alive it still moved. She was willing to let them explore anything that interested them both through the use of cultural tools and through direct experience.

Carlina Rinaldi, writing about the early years provision in Reggio Emilia, tells us that they talk of the *competent child* and they *listen* carefully to the theories children come up with as they struggle to construct meaning through their interactions and experiences. She believes that very young children's early theories are not evidence of naïve thinking or mistaken thinking but evidence of the young child's continual questioning which leads to the search for answers, and which, in Rinaldi's terms, is an aspect of creativity. It is really worth thinking about that. She goes on to say that the competent child is competent because she is perceived as being competent by the significant adults in her world. *Expectations*, then, become an important aspect of scaffolding – of pedagogy itself. In Reggio Emilia they talk often of the *'pedagogy of relationships and listening'*, which, as you can see, takes us back to Vygotsky's view of all learning being social, culture-bound and involving the continuing search, with others, for meaning and significance. A theory, then, becomes a possible and satisfactory explanation for something, albeit one that is provisional.

Rinaldi (2000: 114) cites two interesting examples of theories developed by young children. The first is a simple one. A child said, 'The weather is born from the storm.' Rinaldi's analysis of this is that the child has made an association and then states it, wanting to be heard but not corrected. The child is conceptualising and wants to share it.

The next is more complex: 'But when someone dies, do they go into the belly of death and then get born again?' Since this theory is in the form of a question it does require a response. The child has put together many elements drawn from her experience and also, perhaps, her own anxieties.

Giving feedback

You may be surprised to find giving *feedback* listed as a tool of teaching and of learning. Perhaps you are more used to reading about it in books about assessment. But since all learning is social it makes sense to consider not only what children say to us but also what we say to them. It makes sense, too, to think about how the comments we make can be regarded as scaffolding in their own right. You know that we are able to remember things and carry images in our minds, drawing on our experiences and interactions, on language and on other symbolic tools. We become able to reflect on these to create new understandings. So we build new understandings on the basis of realising what we have understood, what we can do, what we have achieved. One of the tools that helps us do this is the feedback we get from someone who is tuned in to what we have been doing. Here are some examples.

The first relates to a child who had been asked to cut out some pictures and arrange them in the 'correct' order to re-tell a story the class has been listening to. The child, Roman, did cut out the pictures and he did arrange them in an order and he did tell a story from his arrangement. The adult's comment during a plenary session was: 'I was so pleased with what Roman did. He spent a long time looking at the pictures before he started cutting them out and then he arranged them in order on a piece of paper and could then tell me a really good story from the way he had organised the pictures. It wasn't the same story that I read you, but it was a very good story anyway.' As feedback to Roman, it is positive and informative. It helps him realise what he had done well but also that he hadn't really done what he had been asked to do but that this did not matter.

Targeted feedback, where there has been some sharing of attention and purpose, enables children to reflect on what they have achieved. Being able to reflect on learning involves being conscious of what was required and what was achieved. Here are some examples of children reflecting on what they can do, sometimes in conversation and sometimes using what Vygotsky called 'inner speech', to give us, through these monologues, an insight into what they understand. They are drawn from Smidt (2005).

1   Josh, playing with cars on a ramp and talking, out loud, to himself: 'Down they go. Ooops! That one was *really* fast. Again. It was fast again. I'll try this one.'
    (Picks up a bigger car).
    'Even faster! I'll do two together.'
    He has assessed the success of his action and drawn a conclusion allowing him to plan his next move. (Puts both cars at the top of the ramp).
    'The yellow one wins. That's because it is so fast!'
    Josh is telling himself what he is doing and what he is learning from what he is doing.

    (Smidt 2005: 54)

You can see how in this example Josh has assessed the success of his venture.

2   The nursery nurse notices that a child has made a very complex model using many different resources. She sits down next to the child and starts a conversation.
    'I love your model. You have used so many different things – egg boxes, toilet roll holders, lids and shiny things. Oh, and look, some buttons.'
    The child, noticing that the adult is really interested and not just asking

questions joins in, saying, 'It took me a long time, you know'.
The adult responds.
'Yes, I noticed that you were busy doing it all morning, I wonder if that was because it was so difficult to fix some of the bits together.'
The child replies,
'I used this strong glue and also some sellotape and Joshua (another child) gave me these ... these ... 'lastic bands and I used those.'
The adult continues,
'Well, you have made a really exciting model with some bits that move. Are you going to take it home?'

(Smidt 2005: 55)

You can see how the child in this example notices that the adult involved is really interested in what the child is doing.

Looking back, looking ahead

In this chapter we have thought about what those working with children can do to help children move from being able to do certain things with help to doing these unaided. Sensitive and alert practitioners foster independent thought and action and intervene appropriately to enable this to happen. In considering how the gap can be bridged between a child's unaided ability and what the child might achieve with aid – the ZPD – we have looked not only at the role of adults but also at that of 'expert others', who might sometimes be children. Let us summarise this:

- We have seen how others can scaffold learning, helping the child move from needing help to being able to do something unaided.
- We have thought about the importance of learner and teacher, whoever they are, being able to become absorbed and involved in thinking about something together and over a long period of time. Educators must be able to infer what it is that children are paying attention to and must not hijack this in order to 'teach' something.
- We have considered how children can become apprentices to expert others in everyday and real life activities. Through this guided participation children become cognitive apprentices.
- We have thought about the importance of children having some investment in what they are doing so that they care about it and want to know more or solve the problem or express their thoughts and ideas.
- We have looked at how, when children teach one another things, they both benefit.
- We have considered the importance of ensuring we provide opportunities for the activities to raise questions in the minds of the learners and allow them to generate their own theories.

- We have looked at how the comments made by teachers and other educators on what children have done and achieved can help children reflect on what they have done and become aware of what they have learned. This leads to metacognition.

Out of all of this we are able to derive some idea of what we, as educators, can do to ensure that the children we work with have the best possible learning opportunities, the most profitable interactions and encounters and the most meaningful care and education. That is where we go in the next chapter.

Glossary

Word or phrase	What it means	Why it is significant
apprentices in thinking	An idea of Barbara Rogoff, who believed that children who were alongside their adults or other experts were able to be apprentices to the thinking of others in their community.	Closely related to scaffolding but embedded in the actual and everyday lives of the learners.
competent child	Underpins the philosophy of the Reggio Emilia provision and, like Vygotsky, focuses on what the child can do today and also what the child might do tomorrow.	How do you feel about this? I hope it is your philosophy too.
dyad	A pair, two people.	
enable negotiation between teacher and learner	To ensure that there is discussion and support between teacher (or more expert other) and learner.	Another feature of scaffolding.
expectations	What you feel the child can do or could do with help.	Closely related to seeing the child as a competent child.

feedback	Giving responses to learners which focus on what they were trying to do, to help them become conscious of what they know, what they can do and also what they still need to learn related to what was being done.	An important teaching tool often not sensitively or supportively given.
intersubjectivity	The shared meaning that people create through their interactions to make sense of aspects of their lives.	An important aspect of all interactions. Where a teacher or other adult interacts with a child without trying to really know what it is that the child is doing, the interaction lacks intersubjectivity and will not result in learning.
intrapsychological	This means what happens inside a learner.	
large format book	A book which needs to be displayed on a stand with text large enough for all to see and which mimics the book on the knee being read to a child phenomenon.	A teaching resource.
metacognitive skills	This means knowledge about knowledge itself. In common-sense terms it means knowing what you know.	A higher order concept.
pedagogy of relationships and listening	The way in which educators in Reggio Emilia describe their philosophy of teaching.	You might want to try this!
reflect on	To think about.	A higher order concept.

sequence support in scaffolding	To offer carefully measured steps of support to take the learner from dependence to independence.	One of the features of scaffolding.
shared reading	A teaching strategy where a large group of children, together with a teacher, read a large format book together.	A teaching strategy.
sustained shared thinking	Where teacher or educator and child are both focused on the same thing and where whatever is being explored is of interest to the child. This means the child can get deeply involved. The child then constructs new meanings and understandings in negotiation with the more expert others.	The current trend in early years education, but firmly rooted in the ideas of Vygotsky.
theory	An idea which appears to be a solution to a problem one has encountered.	A higher order concept.
transmission of culture	The way in which the values and customs and ideas of a culture are passed on from one generation to another.	Vygotsky was interested in the transmission rather than the acquisition of knowledge.

Chapter 9

What we have learned
A summary

In this chapter we bring together the many strands of this book and weave them into what we might call principles of sound pedagogy, illustrating most of them with at least two case studies. One of these will generally refer to young children and the other to older children so that we begin to see the universality of using Vygotsky's ideas as the foundation of pedagogy. We don't address the last principle because that is the subject of this whole chapter – indeed the subject of this whole book.

Proposed principles of pedagogy

1   All learning is social: the roles of others in learning cannot be ignored.

Social, in this sense, refers to more than the presence of others. It refers to the previous experiences of the learner and the use of socially and culturally constructed tools. The others may be teachers, other adults, and/or more experienced others, who could well be peers or older children. For the educator the importance of this is to ensure that opportunities for interaction between children and between children and adults are planned for and exploited.

2   Knowledge of and respect for cultural values and cultural tools is vital to successful learning.

This implies that all involved in learning/teaching enterprises have to take time and effort to know what experiences and cultural tools their learners have had and ensure that, wherever possible, they have access to using these.

3   Building a culture within the class or setting is important in developing the principles you bring to your teaching.

This will allow you, with your learners, to develop an ethos that values sustained shared attention, respect for one another and the use of shared cultural tools, in an environment in which questioning, seeking answers, making things and having a go are embedded. You are trying to create a culture of learners and learning.

4   Language is the supreme but not the only cultural tool essential in planning and organising learning environments.

Educators must plan for the use of spoken and written language and other symbolic systems or 'languages'. The impact of this is to allow children to use their first language where this is the language in which they hold some concepts (both everyday and in some cases scientific) and to offer opportunities for all children to explore and represent things in ways other than in words. All communicable systems are rule-bound, and inventing and using rules is an important ingredient in becoming able to develop higher order concepts.

5   Learning takes place through experience.

The educator must plan and resource activities which are accessible and meaningful to the children. For the younger children activities should offer first-hand and direct experience to allow for the development of everyday concepts, and all children should have opportunities to create and use symbols, which should enable or enhance their ability to think abstractly. Some of those writing on Vygotsky's work use the term activity theory to refer to learning through experience.

6   There are many ways or modes of learning and all need to be considered.

For younger children, play – in which they are able to follow their own interests and create their own rules – may well be a dominant mode of learning but there are others to be considered. The search is always to find something which will motivate children, offer them a cognitive challenge, and allow them to get deeply involved in what they are doing and to build on what they already know. Listening to stories or making music or expressing ideas through art or drama are all powerful ways of learning as are climbing, sharing, negotiating and, vitally, questioning.

7   There are many ways or models of pedagogy or teaching, most of them closely linked to the ideas of Vygotsky and particularly to his notion of the ZPD.

The gap between what the child can do unaided and what the child might do with help is the zone of proximal development. When the child is helped or makes a leap in learning to bridge this gap, this is described in various ways. Where a more expert other helps the novice take the steps to be able to move ahead from dependence to independence we call this scaffolding. But there are many other modes of teaching, such as listening, making and sharing meaning, observing, giving feedback, modelling, answering, offering resources and so on. All of these should be considered in planning and review. We don't consider here very didactic styles of teaching because these are primarily controlled by adults and not dialogic or interactional or reciprocal and hence not social. They do not fit into the paradigm we are considering.

Principles into practice

In this section we look at some examples drawn from practice and from the literature in order to illustrate these principles of good practice. As you read through them you will find considerable overlap between them and you will also find that most, if not all, represent styles of teaching and learning that you are familiar with. What you may not be so familiar with is the language used to describe and analyse them.

1 All learning is social: the roles of others in learning cannot be ignored

Case study 1.1

The researchers Brown and Palincsar (1988) developed a *reciprocal teaching* system which was social, cooperative and related to the teaching of reading. It does not refer to teaching children *to* read but rather to teaching them to understand a complex text. The process usually involves small groups of about two to seven learners, one of whom assumes the role of 'teacher'. The approach would not really be appropriate for younger children. In the example cited this is what happens. The group reads a passage silently and then the group member who has chosen to be 'teacher' asks a question. Discussion follows, and at some stage the teacher summarises what has been said and the group then moves on to the next paragraph. Someone else in the group then becomes the teacher. The reciprocal roles involve the following four processes:

1. the teacher or another member of the group *summarising* the piece of text, which means identifying the main theme in the text and where necessary explaining it in simpler terms;
2. members of the group *generating questions*;
3. any member of the group responding in order to *clarify* ideas or concepts;
4. all *predicting* and *hypothesising* what might come next, using the text to help them.

Here, with thanks to Palincsar and Brown, is an extract from a discussion regarding a text on geology, which reads as follows:

> Below the crust is a large layer called the mantle. It is a much heavier layer.

The part of the mantle just below the crust is a strange place. Pressure there is very great and the temperatures are very high.

Doug: This told about the second layer of the earth, the one that is under the first one ...
Sara: The one under the crust.
Doug: Yeah, the crust. It told about what it is like, like how heavy it is and what the temperature is. My prediction is that they will tell us about the next layer because this picture [not shown] shows another one, and I'll bet it will be cooler because dirt gets colder when you dig.
Chris: That doesn't make sense to me because, because as it's been goin' down, it's been getting hotter.
Stephanie: And heavier too.
Chris: Pretty soon, we'll get to the gooey stuff and it's real hot.
Sam: That's the lava.
Teacher: Well, let's read on and see who's right in their predictions. What will the next layer be like? Who will be the teacher?
(Palincsar and Brown 1988: 57; cited in Daniels 2001: 110–11)

This is an interesting model and we can see that one of the group, Doug, starts by summarising what they have read. Sara then provides the correct terminology, and Doug comes up with a theory which Chris challenges. The analysis offered by Daniels is that the children are able to support one another's thinking through using the principles of summarising, generating questions, clarifying and predicting – all higher order concepts. Palincsar and Brown believe that the thinking skills being developed through this approach make the learners into excellent scaffolders. This is very close to Paolo Freire's idea of what he called dialogic teaching. He worked throughout his life as an adult educator, primarily in the realm of developing adult literacy and he believed that teaching had to be reciprocal, be about real issues and involve the construction of meaning.

Case study 1.2

Pat Gura was involved in the Froebel Blockplay Project and wrote a book about her findings, *Exploring Learning: Young Children and Blockplay* (1992), which is full of delicious examples of children's thinking as they engage in play with wooden blocks. The first example given here is of two children engaged in reflecting on a construction made by of one of them. Ellie is five and a half years old and she has made a three-dimensional house where she has tried to make integral windows on three adjacent walls. Gura tells us:

She had great difficulty in maintaining the same overall height for all three walls. At one point she had two out of the three with matching walls and windows, with the third finishing several rows of blocks higher. Stephanie pointed this out to her: 'Hey, Ellie ... low, low, high.' Ellie's solution to this novel situation ... was localized. She began to take down the low wall adjacent to the higher one. When the adult asked what she had in mind, Ellie said she had to take it down to build it again 'only high this time'. Having dismantled one of the two lower walls she was left with two parallel walls, one higher than the other, and could not make up her mind whether they were any longer related. 'How can I do it?' she wondered aloud and, without waiting for advice, announced: 'I know! Take 'em all down and no one's got to use 'em (blocks) 'cos I'm going to build it all again.' Whereupon she dismantled the remaining walls and started again.

(Gura 1992: 83)

The researchers provided the children with materials which they knew were open-ended and intrinsically appealing to children because they could play with them in any way they chose. Most of the play was structural and involved construction and de-construction. Some imaginative play arose once the construction had taken shape. Many issues arose in their play and some of these suggested questions for the children to answer and puzzles for them to solve. The above example illustrates a child interacting with another child and with an adult. It is the other child's comment that caused Ellie to stop and evaluate her work. She could see what was wrong but her only solution was to destroy everything she had made and start over again. Perhaps this reminds you of Jacques setting the table one plate at a time until he had internalised the concept of 'three' (see page 32).

In the next example drawn from Gura we find Ellie, again, trying to cope with another problem in one of her structures. This time she was supported in a different way by slightly older Edmund.

She found one side of the 2 × 1 rectangular enclosure she was constructing wandering diagonally towards its opposite number, and complained: 'I can't get this line straight. It keeps going in.' Edmund ... pondered a moment before commenting: 'It is straight ... it's straight across.' He mimed a diagonal by raising his right arm and sweeping it across his body and to the left. 'It's got to be straight down, like this other side.' 'Parallel' is mimed with both arms.

(Gura 1992: 82)

This is an example of *peer teaching*. Edmund is the more expert other in this exchange, and when he adopts the role of 'teacher' and tries to explain the complex understanding he has of geometry he does the best he can to show what he knows. It is obvious from his words and his action that he has really grasped the problem. What he lacks is the specific language of geometry. He does not yet know the words 'diagonal' or 'parallel'. But how wonderfully he is able to convey his meaning and give an explanation for Ellie's problem.

2 Knowledge of and respect for cultural values and cultural tools is vital to successful learning

We know that this principle is about you, the educator, coming to know as much as you possibly can about the cultures and languages of the children in your group or setting and using this knowledge to inform your practice. So anyone entering your room would immediately know that the children in your room belong to different groups or communities, all with differing values and ideas and practices. The activities you offer, the topics you introduce and the resources you use will all reflect this, as will the relationships you set up with parents and carers in the community. Perhaps the key word here is respect.

Case study 2.1

Carmel is a trained nursery teacher who is bilingual. She speaks, reads and writes both Spanish (her first language) and English. She has lived in Manchester for many years but has never forgotten how difficult it was for her and for her parents when they first came here. She is determined that the children she teaches should encounter fewer misconceptions about languages and cultures than she did and so she takes trouble to plan carefully to ensure that diversity becomes something to celebrate. This is what she said in a recent discussion with me:

> We are a team of three. I am bilingual, and so is Amina who is the nursery nurse. She speaks Gujarati and English. The other member of our team is a teaching assistant called Paulina and she is Muslim by marriage but not bilingual. We are in an urban area and our children come from many different backgrounds, homes, cultures and ethnic groups. I always say we are 'the world in a classroom'! We make it our business to know what languages are spoken in the homes of all our children and try and find out as much as we can about their lives before nursery. Did they go to playgroup? Do they go to the mosque? Do they like books and stories? Are they scared of dogs or of the dark? We try to get to know the parent or parents and often call in other people from the community to interpret or translate to ensure we can communicate.
>
> But let me tell you what our room looks like. We are in a school and only have one room and access to a playground, of course. So we carefully plan activities that we think will interest and challenge children, allow them to build on what they have experienced before and which will offer lots of opportunities to play together with others. There is always sand and always water and always some malleable material (and always things in or with them to allow for exploration and we definitely don't change the things in the sand and water on a daily basis.) The reason for this is that we want the children to be able to get deeply involved so things stay there until the play gets static and then we introduce something just slightly different. That is so there is something that looks or seems different and that will raise questions in the

minds of the children. This is one of our primary aims. So, for example, we might decide that after having a scoop in the sand, we might put in a teaspoon. A change in scale and possibly in function might provoke a change in thinking and in play. And the change is small enough to allow for the children to build on what they have been doing with the scoop.

We always provide a big area for domestic home play and might sometimes offer complete sets of things (dolls and clothes and cots or chairs and plates and knives and forks) if we feel the children are interested in counting or matching. We don't have many dressing-up clothes (a conscious choice to avoid stereotyping boys and girls or styles of dress). Instead we have lengths of fabric and the children do the most amazing things with them.

We provide lots and lots of books and these include picture books, flap books, Big Books, story books, books we have made and books in other languages – and story props. These are so important in allowing the children to play at creating or re-creating the meaning of stories or songs or re-enacting, in safety, their own concerns. These things are both indoors and out. We have other areas too, but just let me tell you about one more. We pay attention to what the children are interested in and then try and set up a specific area to meet that need. We have had a gym (lots of mums one year were going to the gym), a hospital, a flower shop, a strange planet, Hogwarts, and lots of others. Here we often introduce specific cultural tools. These may be graphic tools or physical tools or other tools. For example, on the strange planet we introduced some tarot-like cards because the children were talking about a programme on the TV called Yu-Gi-Oh where cards can make magic. [This is an example of practitioners using popular culture to draw all children into the culture of the classroom which they are involved in constructing. You can read more about it later in this section.]

We also plan carefully where adults will be and what they will be doing. We think about what they will be looking and listening for. For us skills of observation and listening are essential for all our adults.

This is only a small part of the very long discussion we had. I then visited the nursery class and was impressed by the feeling it had of a community in its own right. One of the children, Willyanna, offered to show me round and told me all about the things that they do and about what she likes and what she is good at. She became the 'host', was confident and communicative, and introduced me to the other children and told them that I had come to learn about 'their class'. This was clearly a place where the cultural experience and languages of the children were both valued and respected.

Case study 2.2

This case study refers to a recent example of a secondary school in London where the Year 7 classes all agreed to do a project on Mozart's opera *The Magic Flute*. The reasons for this were fascinating and had little to do with Mozart or with 'high' culture. The school had a thriving percussion group and a burgeoning brass band but little else in the way of live music, and when one of the parents came into the school and told a teacher about a version of the opera being done by a South African group, with an orchestra made up of marimbas, percussion, glass bottles and trumpets, she was determined that the children should see it. The production, called *Impempe Yomlingo*, was a triumph of cultural fusion: a European opera translated into an African setting, using the sounds of African instruments and voices. Although about 70 per cent of it was in English there was enough Xhosa to seem familiar to some students and, with its characteristic click sounds, strange and fascinating to others. More than that, the story suddenly made sense when placed in a context where magic creatures and rituals are part of the culture. The Year 7 pupils included many whose families came from Africa and a few who came from Southern Africa but the pulsing music and the dramatic images spoke to all the children. Here is part of the discussion they had back at school.

Johan: My dad has got a CD of it and I can't listen to it. It's boring, but here the music was … yeah, well, cool.
Becky: I like the real music. We went to see it once, but this was just great because it was … it was so, like, for people like us.
Teacher: What made it for people like you?
Henry: Well, we could imagine playing those piano things.
Teacher: Marimbas
Henry: Yeah, marimbas. How do they make those things produce all those notes? And the glass bottles and the drums. And I just loved it when they had those trials to do to show they were good people. Walking on fire and all that.
Abiola: That was good. And some of it was so funny, like those girls and their teddy bear.
Nandi: What about the Queen of the Night? She was well wicked!
Becky: I loved the two love stories – Pamina and Pamino and Pappagena and Pappageno.
Tess: I want to write a love story like that – set here.
Martha: We could. We could do one together.
Johan: Some of the music made me really happy and … I don't know, jiggy! And some of it was really serious and deep and sad.
Teacher: Could you be persuaded to go and see the real opera, do you think?
Johan: Maybe, if someone took me. Maybe, but I think it is very long and I might be bored. I would like to do our own opera here. We could make instruments and Tess and Martha could write the story.

The educators in this example chose to take their children to something which would entertain and challenge them and allow them to use their own cultural tools to engage with those of another culture. In their dialogue back at school you can see how they were relating their own interests and concerns to those seen in the theatre and the discussion ended in a tentative plan to write and produce their own opera. What came of that is not known, but it was certainly a project teachers with energy and initiative could have taken forward.

Case study 2.3

Perhaps some of the most powerful examples come from people who are thinking about what they call *popular culture*, by which they mean the culture of the day. Supreme among those who have written about this is Anne Haas Dyson (1997) who was interested in how children use the tools of popular culture (television, video, DVD, computers, Wii, comics, superheroes and more) both to understand the world and also to come to shared meanings with their peers through negotiation. She was drawn into working with a newly qualified teacher, Kristin, and her second grade class. This research took place in the USA. She found evidence that Kristin recognised the importance of superheroes in the lives of some of the children and she encouraged them to bring this '*cultural capital*' (Bourdieu, 1973) into their own writing. She also set up what she called the Author's Theatre, which was a sort of public forum where the child authors could present their texts and choose peers to act them out. This practice encouraged the children to bring into the classroom what they played at out of school. Dyson followed Kristin as she moved up to third grade and, in analysing what she saw and heard, built on the work of Bakhtin (1981, 1986). He believed that learning to use language (which is a cultural tool) involves learning to interact with others, and through this learning children become familiar with the words and concepts available to those peers who may have had different, and possibly more school-friendly, experience. In this classroom writing itself became play. As composers of stories the children invented characters and situations to explore the 'what if' or 'as if' that they also explore in pretend play. Dyson's book makes for fascinating reading.

3 Building a culture within the class or setting is important in developing the principles you bring to your teaching

Much has been written about the way in which children come to be able to live in several 'worlds' at the same time. Gregory *et al.* (2004) use the term *syncretic* to describe what they call the *creative transformation of culture*. What they mean by this is how people, including children, reinvent culture, drawing on their resources, old and new. The syncretic approach suggests the following three points:

1   All children are members of different cultural and linguistic groups and actively seek to belong to these groups in a way which is not *linear* but is dynamic, fluid and changing.
2   Children do not remain in the separate worlds defined by their cultural group, but move between these worlds. According to Kenner and Kress

(2003) they live in *'simultaneous worlds'*. So a child who is a member of the cultural group of her family is also actively creating the cultural group of her setting or classroom.

3 As children become members of different groups they syncretise, or transform/change the languages and narrative styles, the role relationships and learning styles appropriate to each group and then transform the cultures and languages they use to create new forms. All of this takes place in interactions and through mediation where the mediators may be other children or adults (Gregory *et al.* 2004: 5).

Case study 3.1

The now famous nursery schools of Reggio Emilia spend time and effort creating a culture of their own. One of the most striking visual features of each of these is the indoor piazza – an open public space, mimicking the squares or piazze present in all Italian towns and cities. This is where people meet to chat, to view one another, to read the newspapers and drink coffee, to play and run and to think and to dream. There is no direct equivalent in this country. In all the nurseries there is just such a meeting place where parents and staff and children gather in the morning and at the end of the day and where children may choose to go at any time. It is easy to see why this is regarded as essential to the building of a culture within a culture. Apart from that there are striking similarities across early years provision in the ways in which children are perceived as competent beings, as seekers after 'truth' and creators of new thoughts and reflection. There are similarities, too, in the ways in which adults interact with one another and with the children. All adults are called 'teachers' and all are recognised as playing a role in the children's learning. There are differences too. In one of the nurseries there is a central atelier or art workshop, full of delicious little collections of found and made objects of interest to the children. In the atelier a resident artist worked throughout the day but the children were free to visit him and talk to him and work alongside him, painting or modelling or drawing. So children have opportunities to be apprentices in learning aspects of their culture using specific cultural tools. It did not surprise me, when I was fortunate to visit this nursery, to see children's art work of the most extraordinary quality: tiny detailed drawings of objects; glowing paintings; group collages; models made using clay and an armature – a specially designed wood and wire support to ensure that the clay models did not collapse during construction.

Case study 3.2

The second case study relates to creating a classroom culture of questioning, making and sharing meaning and reflection. This refers to a class of children aged between seven and nine and to the use of drama as a tool for creating what

Grainger (2003) calls *metaxis* – a set of higher order functions which allow the learner to hold the ideas of the real and the possible, the actual and the 'as if' in mind. Can you see the links between this and pretend play?

The children were drawn into a drama session when a known teacher appeared in the role of police officer, wanting more information about a fictional member of the class called Lucy who had not been seen since the previous day. The teacher skilfully drew the children into the scenario, gathering information about Lucy from them and then finding a note which said 'I'm fed up with her, FED UP!'. All of this was suggesting possible events and relationships and the children – almost all of them – got involved. But one group remained sceptical and could not suspend disbelief, so, when the drama teacher left, one of the group spoke anxiously to one of the teaching assistants about the safety of Lucy, and the integrity of the 'police officer'. To deal with this teachers began a discussion about drama and imaginary worlds and explained to the children about the possibility of holding differing views in their heads at the same time. Over time the children began to suggest the presence of 'Lucy's teacher' in order to try and explain the mysterious and angry note. They named her Linda, and she was presented as a malign figure. But discussing this in front of their own teacher presented them with difficulties and embarrassment, wonderfully expressed by one of the pupils, Jack, who said: 'It didn't seem quite right, I mean I know Linda's not Miss Arnold, but it felt difficult – you know.' If you want to know more about this and about the powerful role drama can play in developing a culture where children can safely explore the possibilities they desire or fear, read the chapter from which this case study is drawn in Bearne *et al.* (2003).

The role of an educationalist is that of creating a culture within the classroom or setting and is an important one because creating a sense of belonging is powerful in building children's self-esteem as well as in helping them understand what it means to share and negotiate, to question and find answers together.

4 Language is the supreme but not the only cultural tool essential in planning and organising learning environments

We have spent some time thinking about language and its role as a cultural tool in helping children come to be able to use symbolic systems. A setting or classroom where activities are bathed in language and where children have access to talking and listening and questioning, as well as to using the first language (where this applies), is essential to good practice. Before the first case study, we ought to consider an approach to learning which is exemplified in the work of Elinor Goldschmied and Sonia Jackson, in *People Under Three: Young Children in Day Care* (1994). They developed the concept of *heuristic play*, which they defined as allowing very young children, in groups, to have definite and regular periods of time with many objects to explore but without any adult intervention. Much is said in their work about the sort of objects children should be given (mostly natural, or made of non-plastic materials) and little about the role of the adult, which they suggest is to do little more than to find and present the objects to the child and to watch what happens. The adult is instructed not to praise or comment or suggest: silence rules except when the play becomes disruptive. This approach was very popular for a while and you may still encounter it together with the popular term *treasure baskets*, which is the name given to the collections of objects given to the children. Although it is certainly true that children will learn through exploring interesting objects, it is worth considering whether the role of the adult here enhances learning. So, by contrast, let us turn our attention to a language-rich environment.

Case study 4.1

The first case study comes from the work of Nigel Hall (1999) and refers to what happened in a reception class where a garage was set up in the classroom with the aim of building the children's use of language, spoken and written. To ground the play setting in a context and give it a history (back to 'sociohistorical') the children had paid a visit to a local garage and then became involved in 'building' their own garage in the classroom, based on what they had seen and the 'notes' they had taken. Remember that the children were only or not-yet five years old, and so the notes they had taken were made up of their own ideas about what should go into them. They created all sorts of signs and notices and instructions, all using their own ideas of writing – which included both alphabetic symbols, pictures and invented symbols. The teacher then introduced the idea that, in order to play in the garage, children had to apply for a job in it. This involved the children in a long discussion of what it meant to apply for a job, and out of this came the realisation that they needed advertisements. When they started planning these, they found that they needed to know just what they were applying for (the job in the garage). If you think about it you will see how they had to continually refer back to everyday concepts in order to engage with the scientific concepts they were encountering through this. After much classroom discussion application forms were designed and placed in the garage area and children could complete them alone, or with help from the adults in the room. This is a small-scale project but one which involved these novice writers in a huge range of types of writing – signs and notices, instructions and forms, and so on. Since all of this was set in the social context of play the children were not anxious about having a go. There was no way of failing.

Case study 4.2

This comes from a fascinating and complex study on how peer teaching and interaction can become powerful tools in helping bilingual children come to understand and use English (an essential cultural tool for academic success in this country) in their learning. The study was carried out by Yuangguang Chen and Eve Gregory (2004) and described the experiences of two children who came from Hong Kong to London. The girls were eight-year-old Wington and ten-year-old Kapo. At the school they started to attend were a few Cantonese children, all born and reared in London. Among them was Yuan, who became Wington's best friend. At first Wington was put in a Year 1 mainstream class for literacy lessons because it was said that she needed 'additional help in her basic literacy skills', but after a few months she became a full member of her own class. Tracing what Yuan did to scaffold Wington's learning is extremely interesting: it included her translating and using their mother tongue; repetition; and shared problem-solving in two languages. We will look at the last of these in more detail, and replicate here the field notes made during participant observation in Wington's literacy class:

> The teaching target today was to get children to understand and practise conjunctions like 'before', 'after', 'since'. The task was practised at two levels: at the first level, dozens of short sentences were given in a list and the children were supposed to make complex sentences (consisting of a main clause and subordinate clause) by matching up conjunction words and short sentences from the list. At the second level children were asked to make sentences of their own by using the given conjunction words. The first level task was easy and with little help from Yuan, Wington grasped the rule and finished matching up all of the words in the list even though she might not know exactly the sentence meaning. After that Wington went on to do the second level task. After struggling for a few minutes, she decided to organize the idea in Chinese and asked Yuan if she could work on these ideas with English equivalents. Yuan seemed very happy with this suggestion as she was struggling with what to write about. Wington then showed Yuan what she wrote in Chinese, and read aloud because Yuan, like most of the British-born Chinese, had only a very limited vocabulary, though fluent in speaking. With the help of Wington, Yuan quickly found the English equivalents for the Chinese expressions and also suggested some changes of different wordings and sentence patterns. The second level task ended with perfect sentences.
> (Chen and Gregory 2004)

In this classroom peer interaction was supported, as was the use of first language when necessary to become able to use the second language effectively. Vygotsky, as you know, believed that the social sharing of a problem or of attention was essential in effective learning and here we see these two little girls being able to exchange ideas using two cultural tools – two different languages. Gregory and Chen tell us that this type of support cannot be described as either scaffolding or guided participation because it is a partnership of equals, both learning through the interaction. But what they agree is essential to the success of this interaction is trust, respect and reciprocity. This is certainly something worth remembering.

5 Learning takes place through experience or activities

You will all have thought about how to provide activities for children which are suited to their ages and interests and cultures. Here we will think a little more about how to build cognitive challenges into activities; how to analyse what you see and hear when the children partake in these activities and use this to inform your planning. We need to emphasise here that this has nothing to do with imposed learning targets. Here, instead of case studies, we offer a series of vignettes.

Activity 1

- *The activity is blockplay.* Jonah, in the nursery, has been playing there every day for well over a week.
- *The cognitive challenge is one he has set for himself.* Each construction he has made has been symmetrical and the staff, through observing him, believe the cognitive challenge for him is to internalise the concept of 'symmetrical'.
- *What the staff decided to do.* Their decision was to ensure they used the word symmetry (a scientific concept) in their responses to him and one of them suggested bringing in a mirror to see if he could use that to aid his concept formation.

Activity 2

- *The activity is play in the graphics area.* Rehana has found long strips of paper in the writing area and taken them over to the coat pegs from which she has carefully and laboriously written down each child's name in a list.
- *The cognitive challenge is one she has set for herself.* One of the nursery workers said she thought that Rehana was using staff as models for creating a register.
- *What the staff decided to do.* The nursery worker said that the next day he would talk to her about her register, but he was aware that she may well be interested in just making a list or in learning how to write lots of names.

Activity 3

- *The activity is a 'making' table,* where one member of staff wanted children to explore wheels.
- *The cognitive challenge was decided by the adult,* to see if the children could use circular shapes provided to make wheels. What happened was that the children used the circular shapes for all sorts of things. None of them put wheels on other shapes.
- *What the staff decided to do.* They decided to start with something they had seen one child doing, which was to use elastic bands to create moving parts.

It seems to me that this issue – knowing what activities to offer, how to embed a suitable challenge, how to analyse what you see and hear in order to use it to inform your planning – is central to the training of all those who work with children, particularly young children. Sadly, there is a recent trend towards imposing targets and standards on children rather than working from what they are concerned with. At the very least it is essential that activities offered should allow children to build on what they already know, to understand the point or purpose of the activity, to use all the tools available to them (from sensory-motor exploration to abstract thinking) and to ensure there are opportunities for talk, raising questions, collaboration, negotiation, trying things out, making up theories and representing findings. You will find these more satisfying than planning for children based on unrelated targets set by someone who doesn't even know the child, and who feels that all children of a particular age should meet the same targets.

6 There are many ways or modes of learning and all need to be taken into account

Many books have been written on this topic alone so here, instead of giving you case studies we will instead think about some ways of learning you need to consider when planning your programme. Many will depend on the ages of the children but some are universal.

Imaginative/pretend play/drama

Children learn to use one thing to stand for another, which leads them into dealing with symbolic systems, so essential for the development of higher concepts. They invent rules. They explore things like 'What if?' or 'As if'. It really incorporates role play where children adopt roles in their play in order to feel what it might be like to be and behave like someone else.

Scientific play

Through the exploration and investigation of objects and situations children begin to pose questions and try things out to try to answer them. They are involved in observing, hypothesising, trying things out, making conclusions and evaluating these. These are the little scientists in action.

Physical play

Here children explore the world on a small and a larger scale, using movements and their senses. This kind of play can embrace both pretend play and scientific play.

The routines of the day

Particularly for younger children an enormous amount of learning can happen when the routines of the day involve interactions with others, language, and other symbolic systems like music and exploration. For older children meal times and outings and time in the playground are all contexts where learning takes place. This is not to suggest that you, the adults, hijack these times but that you are aware that learning does not stop when the children go out of the room.

Appreciating

Children spend much time looking at and listening to things – primarily computers or games screens or television. As they watch they are often deeply involved and engaged and they are learning a great deal. Their interactions may be with a screen or an object like a book, but it is possible to view and use these seemingly passive situations to encourage children to think about, question, reflect on and represent what they see and hear. Think about hearing stories read aloud, listening to music, watching moving images or examining still images. All of these are cultural tools and children need exposure to them so that they can both use them to mediate their own understanding and develop more such tools of their own.

Representing

Loris Malaguzzi talked of children having 'a hundred languages' and by this he meant that children have many, many ways of representing what they feel and think about their world and their experiences in it. So children need to have access to tools to allow them to paint and draw and model and make; to make music using their voices and bodies and instruments; to commit their thoughts to paper through writing; to use their bodies in dance; and to play out roles and situations through drama.

Looking back, looking ahead

This chapter is an important one and one that you might turn to again and again when considering the complex and important role of educators. We have tried to bring together the main themes of this book to draw up a set of principles of good practice and then added some case studies to illustrate these principles in action.

The chapter that follows is the last in the book and it takes a look at the work Vygotsky and some of his peers did with children defined as having special needs. At the time he was writing these needs were defined primarily as physical needs but with his total focus on the social nature of all learning he looked also at how the particular physical conditions caused the children to be viewed in particular ways and thus treated as different, other and often as inferior. In his view it was this social and cultural response as much the actual physical conditions that caused these children to struggle in educational settings. A focus on all children seems an appropriate ending to this book.

Glossary

Word or phrase	What it means	Why it is significant
dialogic	This refers to the sort of teaching where teacher and learner are partners and the curriculum or what is learned is negotiated and the learner plays an active role in learning.	This more clearly suits the kind of social/cultural/interactive ideas of Vygotsky.
didactic	This refers to instruction or teaching where the teacher holds the information and 'fills the child' up with it.	It is impossible to see where the ideas of Vygotsky would sit with such a view of teaching.
dynamic	This means changing in response to circumstance.	
heuristic play	The exploration of objects without any verbal support from others.	
linear	This means straightforward, without deviations.	
popular culture	This refers to the culture which is currently popular and as you can imagine this changes over time. Popular culture today might include *Big Brother*, the music of Amy Winehouse, *Pop Idol* and so on.	You should make reference to this in your teaching if you are to make things relevant to the children.

simultaneous worlds	We are all capable of inhabiting different worlds at the same time – hence simultaneous worlds. So a child can be a pupil, a friend, a patient, a helper and so on.	Important to remember this when you think of the activities you might provide.
treasure baskets	These were invented by Elinor Goldschmied and were collections of natural and made objects for young babies to explore.	

Chapter 10

Vygotsky's children

Dan was six years old when he was in my class at an inner London school. He had been with that cohort of peers since the nursery and was very much one of them. They played with him, wiped his tears when he fell, laughed when he clowned around (which was a common response to feeling not equal to some task), pointed to him with affection when he stood beside me to 'read' and while doing that gently pulled on the hairs on my upper lip. Despite his obvious difficulties, physical and cognitive (he had been diagnosed as having Down syndrome), he was a full and active member of this little community. He was very keen to learn to read and would sit on the fringes of any group where someone was reading, and by the end of the year he had learned to decode. He could recognise some words (his name, words with particular significance for him, and he had learned the sounds that some letters make alone or in pairs or groups) but even putting all of this together he could do no more than 'bark at print'. The meaning evaded him. His mother, who had been very happy with his progress, particularly his emotional and social progress, decided the time had come for him to go to a special school. She felt he needed lower ratios, specially trained staff and more adapted technology. She was a teacher.

That same year Noor arrived from Iraq. She had lived in a village, and had never been in a car or on an aeroplane, never lived in a city, never heard English. Two days after arriving in this country she appeared at the school. No one in her family spoke English and we had no one to interpret or translate for her, but we asked another little girl to look after her. Soraya had arrived as a newcomer and a non-English speaker some months earlier. We thought the odd smile or hug or exchange of meaning between the two little girls might take place. Very slowly Noor got drawn into the life of the classroom. At first she sat at the edge of all activities – silent, but watching intently. She would not join in any activities until one day a parent came in to bath her new baby in front of the children. Noor was mesmerised by all that happened and she smiled, for the first time. The next day she spontaneously went and got some paper and drew a picture of the baby being bathed, showed it to one of the adults and spoke out loud. We did not understand what she said but her drawing spoke for her. Three months later the headteacher decided to call in the educational psychologist. She felt that lack of English was holding Noor back and that she needed specialist help. Her proposal was for the child to be put into a withdrawal group to have 'fast track' English lessons. We felt Noor's needs were only special in the way the needs of all children were special and that her learning of English would take place most effectively through remaining with her peers and using English with them.

These two case studies show children who demonstrate something which might give cause for concern in terms of their learning and development. Dan had been diagnosed with a recognised medical syndrome, but Noor's difficulties were purely caused by lack of experience of something very specific. You need to decide whether you think either or both these children can be categorised as having 'disabilities'. The ways in which we define which children have special needs and which not varies over time and according to the views of 'normality' that operate within cultures. For Vygotsky children with behavioural or emotional difficulties were rarely regarded as posing problems. But those with physical or cognitive difficulties fell into the paradigm known as *defectology*.

We now turn our attention to the work Vygotsky did with such special children. He worked primarily with children whose difficulties included being visually impaired or blind, having hearing difficulties or deafness, or speech and language impairment. But he also worked with children who had been orphaned during and after the October Revolution and those suffering the consequences of malnutrition, enforced relocation and lack of education. The term given at the time to this study was, as we have indicated, defectology. This, you will realise, is a term that is no longer acceptable anywhere. The term came from the Russian and meant the study of defects. We cannot make the term 'special needs' its equivalent because defectology did not include children with learning or emotional difficulties.

Biology and culture

To understand Vygotsky's involvement with the study of these children we, as always, have to take account of his sociohistorical theory of human development. You will remember that this meant his focus on the importance of history and culture in his analysis of learning and development, both always rooted in the social. We also need to learn something of his theory of *disontogenesis* – which was the word he used to describe what he saw as 'distorted' development. It will not surprise you to learn that he was ahead of his times in thinking that the problems he saw in the children were not only physical problems but also, more importantly, the problems that others had in responding to them. So although blindness and deafness, for example, are clearly biological in origin, what teachers have to do is to deal *not* with the biological factors in isolation but with their social consequences. At the time this was revolutionary thinking.

In writing about such children Vygotsky felt that there were two lines of development: one natural and the other cultural. These are not new ideas to us. We know that children change physically as they grow older: this is *natural development*. So the word 'natural' here is not used in the sense of being the opposite of artificial but in the sense of being biological. Children change emotionally and cognitively as a result of their interactions and the use of cultural tools: this is *cultural development*. He said that these axes applied not only to the development of special children but to all children. He proposed the following:

- At one end of the spectrum of natural development were those whose cognitive and social functions had been delayed. These children could be considered as retarded (his word, not mine).
- At the other end were those whose cognitive and social development were highly advanced.
- At the same time the other axis, the cultural axis, ran from what he called *primitive* to highly developed cultural functions.
- A child with normal or even highly developed natural abilities (which might include things like spontaneous attention, the ability to memorise and solve problems and so on) might be deprived of the important symbolic tools offered by their culture. This deprivation caused behaviour or a syndrome which he called *primitivity*.

This word might make you feel quite unsettled, as it does me. But here is a case he gives as an example:

> A colleague of his, named Petrova, had worked with a child whose behaviour was characterised by Vygotsky as primitive because when she had been asked how a tree and a log differ, she had replied that she couldn't tell because she had never seen a tree. When a tree outside the window was pointed out to her she said, 'Oh, but that is a linden.'

Vygotsky's explanation for this was that the child had not had opportunities to use language as a tool of reasoning. She was still operating at the level of being able to name but not group or classify or generalise. According to his thesis, illustrated below, the child might have had what he would have called normal abilities but might have missed out on opportunities to use particular cultural tools.

You will find, in Figure 10.1, a diagram adapted from Daniels *et al.* (2007) to illustrate the possible effects and combinations of the two axes of natural and cultural. I find this an extremely crude way of looking at development and my quarrel is not only with the language used (e.g. primitivity) but also with the way in which it has been used. In fact commentators on Vygotsky's work have noted that, after his death, the cultural aspects of his work, potentially so powerful, were neglected and studies focused on individual children and were interpreted without an analysis or understanding of the importance of culture. More recently Feuerstein *et al.* (1978) placed the concepts of cultural difference and cultural deprivation at the heart of their theory of special needs. They were trying to find ways of providing quality education for immigrant children into Israel and attributed the children's difficulties to upheaval, loss of family, loss of identity,

	High cultural development	High natural abilities and high cultural development
Slow natural development compensated for by the use of cultural tools	Normative natural development and normative acquisition of cultural tools	High natural ability amplified or enhanced by acquisition of cultural tools
Slow natural development matched by cultural primitivity	Normal natural development with cultural primitivity	Culturally primitive with high development of natural functions

Figure 10.1 The possible effects and combinations of the two axes of natural and cultural. Adapted from Daniels et al. (2007)

deprivation and dislocation. There is much that is deeply worrying in all of this and it relates to the notion that privileged people in the world can make value judgements about the cultures and cultural tools of others. Because a child has a language we don't know or recognise, comes from an oral rather than a literate culture, or has never been to school, does not mean that this child has anything that prevents her from learning, developing and thriving. But let us return to some less unsettling aspects of the work.

Disontogenesis

At the time Vygotsky was involved with children with special needs the prevailing ideas were that a child who was blind, for example, was just like a normal child without vision; a child who was deaf was just a normal child without hearing. This is a *subtractive* view, as you can easily see, and for Vygotsky it was far too simple to be an acceptable analysis. In his words, 'A child whose development is impeded by a defect is not simply a child less developed than his peers, but is a child who has developed differently' (Vygotsky 1993: 30). So a blind child cannot see but has developed other senses to compensate, perhaps. The child has also been treated in a particular way by parents, family members, doctors, schools and so on. For Vygotsky there were two considerations:

- a primary defect, which is an initial sensory, organic or neurological dysfunction or impairment which negatively affects the child's natural development;

- the consequent secondary effect, which is the way in which the child's impairment affects the interactions which in turn affect the mediation.

The impairment leaves a lasting, sometimes even permanent stain on the child's development

Following on from this explanation he turned his attention to what others could do to assist a child so affected. His remedy was to focus on the development of higher order functions so that even though it is the physical or the natural or biological that may be affected (hearing loss, poor vision, lack of muscle function) the *treatment is the development of the cognitive skills through using cultural tools*. So children who suffer from such deprivation are to be helped to learn to develop abstract reasoning, logical memory, voluntary attention and goal-directed behaviour. Vygotsky called these strategies *compensatory* and he was insistent that a physical impairment of one organ did not necessarily imply a similar impairment of higher order skills.

Let us contextualise this by considering the true story of one particular child. Luigi was born with some mild hemiparesis – weakness of the right side of his body. The doctors told his parents that this was a neurological defect which could potentially affect his motor development. The parents spent a great deal of time talking to specialists about what they could do to minimise the effects of this on the child and on his own self-image. In the early years the parents insisted that he be part of groups with his siblings and cousins and friends. He went to a nursery where he joined in and was so much part of the group that no one noticed his slight clumsiness. When he was about to start formal schooling his parents consulted a psychologist for advice on how to ensure that he did not experience failure which would damage his self-image and his confidence. One of the psychologists they saw told them that they could certainly help him with his gross and fine motor skills and suggested some aids which might help him. One of these was a computer, to allow the development of fine motor skills through doing things that interested him. Using graphic tools like pencils and crayons and paintbrushes was difficult so they talked to Luigi's first teacher and she listened carefully and offered him specially adapted tools to use in the classroom. Outside he was encouraged to kick a ball with his older brother, to go along with his mother to a t'ai chi class, to strum on a guitar, and to be part of groups. All of these activities used cultural tools (adapted graphic tools, a football, a musical instrument, a computer keyboard, a mouse, and so on) and gave him not only the physical skills but also the cognitive and verbal functions to allow him to be part of mainstream schooling

Had Vygotsky known Luigi and his family he would certainly have recognised that it was the role of social mediation and the acquisition of cultural tools that allowed Luigi to live and learn alongside other children in mainstream settings. For Vygotsky the way in which adults are able to think about the world and understand has come about because, as children, they spontaneously acquired mental representations through everyday activities, supported by the use of cultural tools. They may have used spades to dig in the sand, gone with mum to take the baby to the clinic, kicked balls with their friends, listened to adults reading aloud, helped set the table, talked to dad about what had happened at school, or listened to their iPods as they walked to see their friends – a rich and varied life of ordinary, everyday, meaningful activities. So when, at school, they started to encounter more abstract concepts and ideas they were able to deal with these because of the store of images they held in their heads and the fact that they knew how to think and call up these images.

Let us think about this on a more personal basis. When you were young you will almost certainly have encountered the concept of 'half' through everyday activities. You may have asked for an apple and your mum cut it in half for you; you may have felt you had to share with a friend and so eaten half each of your snack bar. By now, if you are planning to bake a cake and the recipe calls for 125g of butter you probably know that all you have to do is take your normal tub of butter, which contains 250g, and use half of that. You know about 'half' through everyday activities and know about the number system partly through everyday activities and partly through schooling. So you know that 250 is made up of 125 and 125.

Now consider this. Many years ago Deanne asked me if I could help her with mathematics. She described herself as 'disnumerate' by which she meant that she had no concept of numbers and how they work. She was a woman in her 40s at the time. She had no identified learning difficulties but had been an evacuee during the war and talked about it as a traumatic and horrific experience – one in which her schooling and her interactions with loved ones were disrupted. As we spent time together I found I had to take her back to handling concrete objects, trying to compensate for the things that had been missed out on in school or had been disrupted during her childhood. So we did a lot of mathematics whilst cooking. On one occasion she was asked to put half a tub of butter into the cake mix. Her solution was to get out a pair of kitchen scales and a teaspoon and to scoop one teaspoon of butter at a time into the bowl of the scales. This was an extremely tedious and laborious process. Deanne was not someone suffering from any physical or cognitive difficulty. Her inability to think abstractly arose from events in her life which had affected her emotional development. When we think of children who have special needs we know that this includes those who have emotional difficulties, but when Vygotsky was writing this was not the case.

Dealing with children with special needs

For Vygotsky the way to help children who had difficulties was not to treat the difficulty itself but rather to treat the effects that the difficulty had caused the child in her relationships and interactions. What Vygotsky proposed was to create alternative ways into cultural development. He felt that if children acquired the cultural tools they would be able to transform their natural abilities into higher mental functions. So the notion of internalisation becomes important here as it does in all development and learning. Vygotsky emphasised the dialectical relationship between the signs or tools and the meaning of what was to be learned or appropriated. Put in everyday language this means that some of the tools need to be adapted to meet the particular needs of the learner in order to enable them to be used. So a child with visual difficulties may need access to enlarged print; a child with a hearing loss needs to be seated at the front of the class; a child with poor motor control needs to use a keyboard rather than a pencil, and so on. But the question arises whether changes in the tools themselves are enough. Vygotsky reminds us that it is the meaning that matters: 'Different symbolic systems correspond to one and the same content of education ... Meaning is more important than the sign. Let us change signs but retain meaning' (1983: 54).

The adaptation of tools has proceeded at a remarkable rate and technology has certainly made things more possible for many learners. But the question remains how these tools can be made to be useful to mediation. Kozulin and Gindis (2007) tell us that in the course of what we might call 'normal' development there is interaction between the everyday concepts children gain through their hands-on experience and the scientific concepts which come about as the result of determined teaching. For children with disabilities this may not be the case. Everyday concepts may be limited or immature and distorted through physical problems (limited sight or hearing or understanding, for example) and that suggests that scientific concepts become more important. This implies that teachers need to consider what is the most effective way of supporting the learning of those with special needs. There is an important message in all of this. To focus on some remediation of the initial problem (loss of sight or hearing, for example) will have less long-term or profound impact than helping the child become able to think abstractly. As Vygotsky himself said, 'Training sharpness of hearing in a blind person has natural limitations; compensation through the mightiness of the mind (imagination, reasoning, memorization, etc.) has virtually no limits' (1983: 212).

The zone of proximal development

It does not require an enormous leap of understanding to appreciate how important the idea of assessment is in terms of children who have special needs. Children who have special needs, like all children, should be assessed in terms of what they know and what they can do. It is only when educators know this that they can plan what the children now need to learn. There are many ways in which children can be assessed, some of which fall into what can be called *dynamic approaches* to assessment. This is based on Vygotsky's view of development which insists that, since higher order mental processes come about through interactions with others and being then internalised, other people are key in stimulating learning. *So learning is constructed jointly, through interactions with adults or peers, and can be enhanced by matching the help offered to the child's interests, current situation and assessed needs.* Tests like IQ tests can be described as *static* (as compared to the dynamic approach indicated above) and tell you only what a learner has learned in the past. What educators need to know is what could the child learn today with the appropriate help. So we arrive at the ZPD again.

Vygotsky believed that static tests focus on the fruits of development rather than on what he called its buds or its flowers. So they measure the end product rather than monitoring the process. He also noted how dependent such tests were on cultural norms. A child who has never seen or heard about snow cannot be expected to demonstrate understanding of things related to snow, for example. Nowadays there is a tendency to use both static tests and dynamic tests, and there is an emphasis on focusing on what the child knows and can do rather than on what the child doesn't know and can't do. The ZPD allows for the fact that a qualitative distinction can be made between those children who may suffer some cognitive impairment and those whose development has been delayed for one reason or another (think of Deanne). The difference lies not in their performance but in their responses to benefiting from the help given during the interaction or scaffolding. *Dynamic assessment is an interactive process which focuses on the strategies the child uses to solve problems and the extent to which the child has benefited from scaffolding.* The child's performance needs to be assessed before the help given and afterwards. Perhaps we need to think more carefully, when working with children who have special needs, about how we group the children and how we might allow for the use of an organised peer group – what Vygotsky called 'a collective'. Such a collective could function as an effective means of mediation and a powerful facilitator in forming the higher psychological function particularly in a child with a disability.

Inclusion

You may well be surprised to learn that Vygotsky was very much in favour of children who had special needs being in mainstream settings rather than in separate groups alongside others with difficulties. This derived from his idea that the development of a child with a disability is determined by the social aspects of her (often physical or organic) impairment. Positive responses will allow for children to be supported, helped and accepted. Taking the child out of the group often causes the child to be negatively perceived and labelled. It took Vygotsky several years to develop his unique vision for the future model of special education which he called 'inclusion based on positive differentiation'. This meant that society must view children with disabilities in terms of their strengths and not of their weaknesses. He was interested in how children could be fully included in their neighbourhoods, cultures, groups and classes as full members. He opposed low expectations, a watered-down curriculum and social isolation. So he was determined that all children should be offered schools and settings where staff were appropriately trained to educate and support them, where a wide and appropriate range of cultural tools was used, and where methods of teaching were matched to the unique needs of each pupil.

His views on integration match those of the regulating authorities of Reggio Emilia. For over 30 years that region has worked towards integrating most of its 'disabled' pupils into mainstream schools, classes and settings. In the nursery schools which have been so often raised in this book as models of aspects of good practice and of the ideas of Vygotsky (even though this is not always explicit) this policy is implemented. This should surprise none of us because of what we have already learned about how important society and culture (and children) are in Italian society and how much attention is given to knowing each child as an individual. Definitions of special needs vary from country to country and in Italy it seems that the children who are included are those with physical impairments, developmental delay and conditions like Down syndrome. Angela Nurse (2001) visited Reggio Emilia and wrote this about her impressions:

> preschool minimizes many of the effects of disability and a slower rate of learning because the learning environment matches the developmental and social needs of the individual child. A number of reflections lead me to consider that perhaps the ethos and practice also limits the development of challenging behaviour. A difference between the systems in the UK and the Reggio response is the commitment to children learning as a group, from each other. The language used by the children was rich … both in the complexity of the structures they used to explain what they were doing and what they understood, but also in exploring difficult concepts, such as war and death (subjects often neatly evaded with young children in much of the UK). The children listened to each other, made suggestions about particular problems encountered in their work, and asked for advice. Adults were there to suggest and support, but not to take away from children the responsibility for solving problems.
>
> (Nurse 2001: 68)

Reading through that you will be struck by how many of the ideas of Vygotsky are included: the narrow range of 'disabilities' constituting special needs; the focus on dealing not only with the actual disabilities but to the reactions of others; matching the programme to the needs of the children; seeing learning as interactive; and recognising the importance of higher mental functions such as problem-solving.

Nurse goes on to make the important point that the schools and nurseries form only a small part of the lives of children. Where and how the children live matters hugely and in Reggio Emilia the community is stable and prosperous and early years care and education are valued. Parents play a central role and staff and parents respect one another and focus on the needs of the child. Extended families often play a role and people are able to meet others in their community out in the squares and restaurants and in the schools or nurseries. Deep engagement in activities is regarded as normal and important. But there are also activities on offer where children can just contribute something 'on the run' – like a weaving loom with a basket of threads beside it, so a child can just weave one row or more in passing. This highlights the importance of attitudes in the community to those with special needs.

Looking ahead

I hope this book has given you some insight into the ideas of Lev Vygotsky and, if you are impressed with these thoughts, offered you some ideas of what you can do as a practitioner to enhance the learning of those in your care. There is much, much more you can read about him and his followers.

Glossary

Word or phrase	What it means
compensatory	This was the term used to describe what Vygotsky thought could be done to make up for (or compensate for) the particular disability.
defectology	The term used by Vygotsky to describe the study of children requiring additional help. They were usually children with some physical or cognitive impairment or children who had suffered some trauma. But emotional and behavioural difficulties were not included.
disontogenesis	The term used by Vygotsky to describe the development of children with special needs which he saw as development that had been disrupted in some way.
primitivity	A disturbing term used by Vygotsky to talk about one end of the continuum he suggested between high culture and its opposite.
subtractive	An approach that saw a child with a disability as being a 'normal' child minus something.

A final word

You have been on a journey with me into the world and ideas of one of the most remarkable thinkers of the last century. Our journey started in the snowy town of Orsha in Russia and moved through to Gomel, Moscow and back to Gomel before looking beyond to how this man has influenced others who worked with him and later who read his ideas. In his short life he lived through pogroms at home, discrimination against him and his peers who were Jewish, the impact of the Great War and the German Occupation, the years of starvation, the Russian Revolution, and the dramatic social and political changes brought by these, and finally the rise to power of Stalin. He died at the very young age of 37 and in that brief and extraordinary life he wrote no less than 15 works, publications which addressed issues ranging among psychology, semiotics, play, adolescence, learning and teaching, children with special needs, literacy, cognition, and more. All his work, as you know, was set in a sociohistorical context and all focused on the ongoing and dynamic contexts of experience, interaction and culture. He is famous for many things, some of which you may already have known about but some of which will almost certainly be new to you. I hope you have found this an engrossing and enriching journey.

It has been a privilege for me to have had the opportunity to write this book about ideas and education at a time when I fear that education has become a system of measuring and weighing children rather than 'feeding' or nourishing them. And as all farmers know, weighing a pig does not make it fatter. Reading the ideas of Vygotsky has taken me back to a time when the children I met and worked with were children who were curious about their world and wanted to find ways of exploring it, describing it, representing it and feeling passionately about it. Seven-year-old Sonay (the names of the children in this chapter have been changed) said to me, 'I love it – I love it so much, when we read long stories and at the end of the class we go home wondering what will happen next.' Four-year-old Franklin would not go home until he had balanced the top block on his tower. Six-year-old Benjamin, who had spent weeks and weeks doing no more than throwing pens up in the air, sang like an angel when we did a child-scale version of *West Side Story*. Five-year-old English-speaking Alice linked her arms with Greek-speaking Eleni and announced, 'She is me, only Greek. We are friends!' And Filiz told me that I should learn to speak Turkish because 'it is beautiful language and it is my language'.

These children were learning through all their encounters and interactions, through language and music and dance and drawing and making things. They were supported by adults who found them interesting and respected their efforts to make sense of the world and who enjoyed working with one another. Many of the children have gone on to be serious learners, thinkers and do-ers. Polat (deported to Turkey with his family) writes serious comic strips; Peter (whose parents ran a takeaway in London) is a doctor working in China; Archana (who struggled to learn to read) has become a teacher; Mariam (who threw temper tantrums on a daily basis) is writing children's books; and Zohra (who had her head in a book all day long) is a psychologist writing her thesis on Vygotsky. For me they are all Vygotsky's children and this book is written in the hope that there will be more of them in the years to come.

Bibliography

Abbott, L. and Nutbrown, C. (eds) (2001) *Experiencing Reggio Emilia: Implications for Pre-school Provision*. Buckingham and Philadelphia: Open University Press.

Bakhtin, M. (1981) 'Discourse in the novel'. In C. Emerson and M. Holquist (eds), *The Dialogic Imagination: Four Essays by M. Bakhtin*, Austin: University of Texas Press.

—— (1986) *Speech Genres and Other Late Essays*. Trans.Vern W. McGee. Austin: University of Texas Press.

Bearne, E., Dombey, H. and Grainger, T. (2003) *Classroom Interactions in Literacy*. Maidenhead: Open University Press.

Berger, M. (2005) 'Vygotsky's theory of concept formation and mathematics education'. In H.L. Chick and J.L. Vincent (eds) *Proceedings of the 29th Conference of the International Group for the Psychology of Mathematics Education, vol. 2*. Melbourne: PME: 153–60.

Blaise, M. (2005) *Playing It Straight: Uncovering Gender Discourses in the Early Childhood Classroom*. New York and London: Routledge.

Boal, A. (2000) *Theater of the Oppressed*, 2nd edn. London: Pluto Press.

Bourdieu, P. (1973) 'Cultural reproduction and social reproduction'. In R. Brown (ed.), *Knowledge, Education and Cultural Change*. London: Tavistock.

Brown, A.L. and Palincsar, A.S. (1989) 'Guided co-operative learning and individual knowledge acquisition'. In L.B. Resnick (ed.), *Knowing, Learning and Instruction: Essays in honour of Robert Glaser*. Hillsdale, NJ: Lawrence Erlbaum: 393–451.

Brown, K. and Cole, M. (1997) 'Fifth Dimension and 4-H: complementary goals and strategies'. *Youth development focus*, 3(4). Davis, CA: University of California Center for Youth Development.

Browne, A. (1996) *Developing Language and Literacy 3–8*. London: Paul Chapman Publishing

Bruce, T. (1991) *Time to Play in Early Childhood Education*. London: Hodder & Stoughton.

Bruner, J.S. (1966) *Towards a Theory of Instruction*. London: Harvard University Press.

—— (1997a) 'Celebrating divergence: Piaget and Vygotsky'. *Human Development*, 40: 63–73

Bruner, J.S., Caudhill, E. and Ninio, A. (1997b) 'Language and experience'. In R.S. Peters (ed.), *John Dewey Reconsidered* (The John Dewey Lectures, University of London). London: Routledge.

Chen, Y. and Gregory, E. (2004) 'How do I read these words?' In E. Gregory, S. Long and D. Volk (eds), *Many Pathways to Literacy: Young Children Learning with Siblings, Grandparents, Peers and Communities*. New York and London: Routledge Falmer.

Clay, M.M. and Cazden, C.B. (1990) 'Scaffolding instruction and implications: a Vygotskian interpretation of Reading Recovery and application of sociohistorical psychology'. In L.C. Moll (ed.), *Vygotsky and Education: Instructional Implications and Applications of Sociocultural Psychology*. Cambridge: Cambridge University Press.

Cole, M. (1985) 'The zone of proximal development: where culture and cognition create each other'. In J.V. Wertsch (ed.), *Culture, Communication and Cognition: Vygotskian Perspectives*. Cambridge: Cambridge University Press.

—— (1996) *Cultural Psychology: A Once and Future Discipline*, Cambridge, MA: Harvard University Press.

—— (2003) 'Vygotsky and context: where did the connection come from and what difference does it make?' Paper prepared for Biennial Conference of the International Society for Theoretical Psychology, Istanbul, Turkey.

Cole, M. and Distributed Literacy Consortium (1996) *The Fifth Dimension: An After-School Program Built on Diversity*. New York: Russell Sage Foundation.

Cole, M. and Wertsch, J.V. (eds) (1995) *Contemporary Implications of Vygotsky and Luria*. Heinz Werner Lecture Series. Worcester, MA: Clark University Press.

Damon, W. and Phelps, E. (1989) 'Critical distinctions among three approaches to peer education'. *International Journal of Educational Research*, 13: 9–19.

D'Andrade, R. (1990) 'Some propositions about the relations between culture and human cognition'. In R. Shweder and R. LeVine (eds), *Cultural Psychology: Essays in Comparative Human Development*. Cambridge: Cambridge University Press.

Daniels, H. (2001) *Vygotsky and Pedagogy*. New York and London: Routledge Falmer.

Daniels, H., Cole, M. and Wertsch, J.V. (eds) (2007) *The Cambridge Companion to Vygotsky*. Cambridge: Cambridge University Press.

Datta, M. (ed.) (2000) *Bilinguality and Literacy: Principles and Practice*. London: Continuum.

—— (2004) 'Friendship literacy: young children as cultural and linguistic experts'. In E. Gregory, S. Long and D. Volk (eds), *Many Pathways to Literacy: Young Children Learning with Siblings, Grandparents, Peers and Communities*. New York and London: Routledge Falmer.

Donaldson, M. (1978) *Children's Minds*. London: Croom Helm.

Dixon-Krauss, L.A. (1992) 'Whole language: bridging the gap from spontaneous to scientific concepts'. *Journal of Reading Education*, 18: 13–17.

Drummond, M.J. (1998) 'Observing children'. In S. Smidt (ed.), *The Early Years: A Reader*. London and New York: Routledge.

Duncan, R. M and Tarulli, D. (2003) 'Play as the leading activity of the preschool period: insights from Vygotsky, Leontiev and Bakhtin'. *Early Education and Development*, 14/3: 270–92.

Dunn, J. (1988) *The Beginnings of Social Understanding*. Cambridge, MA: Harvard University Press.

Durant, A., Ochs, E. and Ta'ase, E.K. (2004) 'Change and tradition in literacy instruction in a Samoan American community'. In E. Gregory, S. Long and D. Volk (eds), *Many Pathways to Literacy: Young Children Learning with Siblings, Grandparents, Peers and Communities*. New York and London: Routledge Falmer.

Dyson, A.H. (1997) *Writing Superheroes: Contemporary Childhood, Popular Culture and Classroom Literacy*. New York and London: Teachers College Press.

Dziurla, R. (n.d.) 'Semiotics of play in view of the development of higher mental functions'. Available online: http://webpages.charter.net/schmolzel/vygotsky/dziurla.html (accessed October 2008).

Elkonin, D. (1995) *Selected Works in Psychology*. Moscow: Pedagogika.
Engeström, Y. (1987) *Learning by Expanding: An Activity-theoretical Approach to Developmental Research*. Helsinki: Orienta-Konsultit.
—— (1999) 'Innovative learning in work teams analysing cycles of knowledge creation in practice'. In Y. Engeström, R. Miettinin and R.L. Punamaki (eds), *Perspectives on Activity Theory*. Cambridge: Cambridge University Press.
Feuerstein, R. (1980) *Instrumental Enrichment: Integrated Programme for Cognitive Modifiability*. Baltimore, MD: University Park Press.
Feuerstein, R., Miller, R., Hoffman, M.B., Minzker, Y. and Jensen, M.R. (1981) 'Cognitive modifiability in adolescence: cognitive structure and the effects of intervention'. *Journal of Special Education*, 15(2): 269–87.
Figueirido, M (1998) '"Tricks"'. In S. Smidt (ed.), *The Early Years: A Reader*. London: Routledge.
Freire, A.M.A. and Macedo, D. (eds) (1998) *The Paulo Freire Reader*. New York: Continuum.
Freire, P. and Macedo, D. (1987) *Literacy: Reading the Word and the World*. London: Routledge and Kegan Paul.
Gleick, J. (1992) *Genius: Richard Feynman and Modern Physics*. London: Little, Brown and Co.
Goldschmied, E. and Jackson, S. (1994) *People Under Three: Young Children in Day Care*. London and New York: Routledge.
Grainger, T. (2003) 'Exploring the unknown: ambiguity, interaction and meaning making in classroom drama'. In E. Bearne, H. Dombey and T. Grainger (eds), *Classroom Interactions in Literacy*. Maidenhead: Open University Press.
Gregory, E., Long, S. and Volk, D. (eds) (2004) *Many Pathways to Literacy: Young Children Learning with Siblings, Grandparents, Peers and Communities*. New York and London: Routledge Falmer.
Griffin, P. and Cole, M. (1984) 'Current activity for the future: the zo-ped'. In B. Rogoff and J.V. Wertsch (eds), *Children's Learning in the Zone of Proximal Development*. San Francisco: Jossey-Bass.
Gura, P. (ed) (1992) *Exploring Learning: Young Children and Blockplay*. London: Paul Chapman Publishing.
Hall, N. (1999) 'Young children, play and literacy: engagement in realistic uses of literacy'. In J. Marsh and E. Hallet (eds), *Desirable Literacies: Approaches to Language and Literacy in the Early Years*. London: Paul Chapman Publications.
Isaacs, S. (1930) *Intellectual Growth in Young Children*. London: Routledge & Sons, Ltd.
Ivić, I.D. (1994) 'Lev S. Vygotsky'. *Prospects*, XXIV(3/4): 761–85.
Jane, B. and Robbins, J. (2004) 'Grandparents supporting children's thinking in technology'. Paper presented at 2004 Annual Conference of the Australian Association for Research in Education, Melbourne: Nov. 28–Dec. 2. Available online at www.aare.edu.au/04pap/jan04113.pdf.
Karmiloff-Smith, A. (1994) *Baby, It's You*. London: Ebury Press.
Katz, L. (1998) 'A developmental approach to the curriculum in the early years'. In S. Smidt (ed.), *The Early Years: A Reader*. London: Routledge.
Kearney, C. (2003*) The Monkey's Mask: Identity, Memory, Narrative and Voice*. Stoke-on-Trent: Trentham Books.
Kelly, C. (2004) 'Buzz Lightyear in the nursery: intergenerational literacy learning in a multimedia age'. In E. Gregory, S. Long and D. Volk (eds), *Many Pathways to Literacy:*

Young Children Learning with Siblings, Grandparents, Peers and Communities. New York and London: Routledge Falmer.

Kenner, C. (2004a) *Becoming Biliterate: Young Children Learning Different Writing Systems.* Stoke-on-Trent: Trentham Books.

Kenner, C. (2004b) 'Community school pupils reinterpret their knowledge of Chinese and Arabic for primary school peers'. In E. Gregory, S. Long and D. Volk (eds), *Many Pathways to Literacy: Young Children Learning with Siblings, Grandparents, Peers and Communities.* New York and London: Routledge Falmer.

Kenner, C. and Kress, G. (2003) 'The multisemiotic resources of biliterate children'. *Journal of Early Childhood Literacy*, 3(2): 179–202.

Kozulin, A. (1999) *Vygotsky's Psychology: A Biography of Ideas.* 2nd edn. Cambridge, MA: Harvard University Press.

Kozulin, A. and Gindis, B. (2007) 'Sociocultural theory and education of children with special needs: from defectology to remedial pedagogy'. In H. Daniels, M. Cole and J.V. Wertsch (eds), *The Cambridge Companion to Vygotsky.* Cambridge: Cambridge University Press.

Lanigan, G. (1998) 'Playing with magnets'. In S. Smidt (ed.), *The Early Years: A Reader.* London: Routledge.

Larkin, M. (2001) 'Providing support for student independence through scaffolded instruction'. *Exceptional Children*, 34(1): 30–4.

Lave, J. and Wenger, E. (1991) *Situated Learning: Legitimate Peripheral Participation.* Cambridge: Cambridge University Press.

Leontiev. A.N. (1978) *Activity, Consciousness and Personality.* Englewood Cliffs, NJ: Prentice Hall Publishers.

―― (1981) *Problems of the Development of the Mind.* Moscow: Progress Publishing.

Levi, P. (1988) *The Drowned and the Saved.* London: Michael Joseph.

Luria, A.R. (1976) *Cognitive Development.* Cambridge, MA: Harvard University Press.

McClaren, P.L. and Lankshear, C. (eds) (1994) *Politics of Liberation: Paths from Freire.* London and New York: Routledge.

Malaguzzi, L. (1984) *L'Occhio Se Salta Il Muro.* Giglio

Marsh, J. and Hallet, E. (eds) (1994) *Desirable Literacies: Approaches to Language and Literacy in the Early Years.* London: Paul Chapman Publications.

Matusov, E. (1998) 'When solo activity is not privileged: participation and internalisation models of development'. *Human Development* 41: 326-49

Meadows, S. (1993) *The Child as Thinker: The Development and Acquisition of Cognition in Childhood.* London: Routledge.

Meek, M. (ed.) (1996) *Developing Pedagogies in the Multilingual Classroom: the writings of Josie Levine.* Stoke-on-Trent: Trentham Books.

Mercer, N. (2000) *Words and Minds: How We Use Language to Think Together.* London: Routledge.

Mercer, N., Wegerif, R. and Dawes, L. (1999) 'Children's talk and the development of reasoning in the classroom'. *British Educational Research Journal*, 25(1): 95–111.

Moll, I.C. (1990) *Vygotsky and Education: Instructional Implications and Applications of Sociohistorical Psychology.* Cambridge: Cambridge University Press.

Newman, D., Griffin, P. and Cole, M. (1989) *The Construction Zone: Working for Cognitive Change in School.* Cambridge: Cambridge University Press.

Nurse, A. (2001) 'A question of inclusion'. In L. Abbott and C.Nutbrown (eds), *Experiencing Reggio Emilia: Implications for Pre-school Provision.* Buckingham and Philadelphia: Open University Press.

Paley, V.G. (1999) *The Kindness of Children*, Cambridge, MA, and London: Harvard University Press.

Palincsar, A. and Brown, A.L. (1984) 'Reciprocal teaching of comprehension-fostering and comprehension-monitoring activities'. *Cognition and Instruction*,1(2): 117–75.

—— (1988) 'Teaching and practising thinking skills to promote comprehension in the context of group problem solving'. *Remedial and Special Education*, 9(1): 53–9.

Pea, R.D. (1993) 'Practices of distributed intelligence and designs for education'. In G. Salomon (ed.), *Distributed Cognitions: Psychological and Educational Considerations*. Cambridge: Cambridge University Press.

Pramling, N. and Samuelsson, I.P. (2001) '"It is floating 'cause there is a hole": a young child's experience of natural science'. *Early Years*, 21(2): 139–49.

Riley, J. (ed.) (2003) *Learning in the Early Years: A Guide for Teachers of Children 3–7*. London: Paul Chapman Publishing.

Rinaldi, Carlina (2006) *In Dialogue with Reggio Emilia: Listening, Researching and Learning*. London: Routledge.

Rogoff, B. (1990) *Apprenticeship in Thinking: Cognitive Development in Social Context*. Oxford: Oxford University Press.

Rogoff, B. and Lave, J. (eds) (1999) *Everyday Cognition: Development in Social Context*, 2nd edn. Cambridge, MA: Harvard University Press.

Rogoff, B. and Wertsch, J.V. (eds) (1984) *Children's Learning in the Zone of Proximal Development*. San Francisco: Jossey-Bass.

Romero, M. E. (2004) 'Cultural literacy in the world of Pueblo children'. In E. Gregory, S. Long and D. Volk (eds), *Many Pathways to Literacy: Young Children Learning With Siblings, Grandparents, Peers and Communities*. London: Routledge Falmer.

Roskos, K.A. and Christie, J.F. (eds) (2000) *Play and Literacy in Early Childhood: Research from Multiple Perspectives*. Mahwah, NJ: Lawrence Erlbaum Associates.

Saussure, F. de (1974) *Course in General Linguistics*. London: Fontana/Collins.

Scribner, S. (1990) 'Reflections on a model'. *The Quarterly Newsletter of the Laboratory of Comparative Human Cognition*, 12(2): 90–4.

Siraj-Blatchford, I., Sylva, K., Muttock, S., Gilden, R. and Bell, D. (2002) *Researching Effective Pedagogy in the Early Years*. DfES Research Brief 356. London: DfES.

Smidt, S. (ed.) (1998) *The Early Years: A Reader*. London: Routledge.

—— (2003) 'Six fingers with feeling: play, literacy and politics'. In E. Bearne, H. Dombey and T. Grainger (eds), *Classroom Interactions in Literacy*. Maidenhead: Open University Press.

—— (2005) *Observing, Assessing and Planning for Children in the Early Years*. London: Routledge.

Smith, M. (1998) 'Let's Make Honey'. In S. Smidt (ed.), *The Early Years: A Reader*. London: Routledge.

Tomasello, M., Kruger, A.C. and Ratner, H.H. (1993) 'Cultural learning'. *Behavioural and Brain Sciences*, 16(3): 495–552.

Van Der Veer, R. (1986) 'Vygotsky's developmental psychology'. *Psychological Reports*, 59: 527–36.

Vygodskaya, Gita (n.d.) 'Gita's reflection on her father L.S. Vygotsky'. Trans. Ilya Gindis. *School Psychology International*, 16.

Vygotsky, L.S (1962). *Thought and Language*. Ed. and trans. E. Haufmann and G. Vakar. Cambridge, MA: MIT Press.

—— (1967) 'Play and its role in the mental development of the child'. *Soviet Psychology*, 5: 6–18.

Vygotsky, L.S (1978) *Mind in Society: Development of Higher Psychological Processes*. Cambridge, MA: Harvard University Press.
—— (1981) 'The genesis of higher mental functions'. In J.V. Wertsch (ed.), *The Concept of Activity in Soviet Psychology*. Armonk, NY: Sharpe.
—— (1987) 'Thinking and speech'. In R.W. Rieber and A.S. Carton (eds), *The Collected Works of L.S. Vygotsky, Vol. 1: Problems of General Psychology*. New York and London: Plenum.
—— (1997) 'Analysis of higher mental functions'. In R.W. Rieber (ed.), *The Collected Works of L.S. Vygotsky, Vol. 4: The History of the Development of Higher Mental Functions*. New York: Plenum Press.
Wells, G. (1985) 'Pre-school literacy related activities and success in school'. In D. Olsen., N. Torrance and N. Hildyard (eds), *Literacy, Language and Thought*. Cambridge: Cambridge University Press.
—— (1986) *The Meaning Makers: Children Learning Language and Using Language to Learn*. Portsmouth: Heinemann.
—— (1994) 'Learning and teaching "scientific concepts": Vygotsky's ideas revisited'. Paper presented at the Vygotsky and the Human Sciences Conference, Moscow, September 1994.
—— (1999) *Dialogic Inquiry: Towards a Sociocultural Practice and Theory of Education*. Cambridge: Cambridge University Press.
Wertsch, J.V. (1981) *The Concept of Activity in Soviet Psychology*. Armonk, NY: Sharpe.
—— (1984) 'The zone of proximal development: some conceptual issues'. In B. Rogoff and J.V. Wertsch (eds), *Children's Learning in the Zone of Proximal Development*. San Francisco: Jossey-Bass.
Williams, A. (2004) '"Right, get your book bags!": siblings playing school in multiethnic London'. In E. Gregory, S. Long and D. Volk (eds), *Many Pathways to Literacy: Young Children Learning with Siblings, Grandparents, Peers and Communities*. New York and London: Routledge Falmer
Wood, D. (1988) *How Children Think and Learn*. Oxford: Blackwell.

Websites

Cultural-historical Activity Theory: http://www.edu.helsinki.fi/activity/pages/chatanddwr/chat/ (accessed 11 March 2008)
A Mediation Model for Dynamic Literacy Instruction: Lisbeth Dixon-Krauss: http://webpages.chater.net/schmolzel/vygotsky/krauss.html (accessed 4 February 2008).
Pierce, C.S. (1839–1914) see Cole: http://www.lchc.ucsd.edu

Index

abstract thinking 27, 102, 119–20, 153
activity 3, 17, 27–30, 33, 37, 60–2, 63–7, 77, 82, 87, 89, 91–6, 101, 103, 105–6, 123–4, 125, 129, 141, 153–4, 172–4; leading 95, 102, 170; meaningful 27; theory 88–101, 130, 171, 174
adapt 13, 44, 48
adults 4–5, 20, 24–5, 29–30, 37–9, 44, 50, 54, 64, 67, 74, 76, 80, 85, 88, 92, 109, 112, 119, 124–9, 135–6, 139, 141, 145, 148, 150, 154, 157, 161–5, 168; adult intervention 149; significant adults 5, 58, 133
agency 2, 17
appropriation of sociocultural practices 98, 116, 118
art 7–10, 18, 33, 53, 128, 140, 148
artefact-mediated 90, 93, 100
artefacts 14, 34, 37, 91, 94
assessment 96, 133, 163–164
assign meaning 12, 14
aware 28, 34, 46–7, 69, 70, 73, 98–100, 125, 136, 152, 154
awareness 6, 13, 15, 17, 43, 54, 67, 68, 70, 74, 98, 128

Bakhtin, M.M. 98–100, 128, 147, 169, 170
Bearne, E. 149, 169, 171, 173
biological processes 24, 47
biology 46–7, 55, 158
Bizos, G. 10
Blaise, M. 99, 169
Boal, A. 169
Bourdieu, P. 18, 147, 169
boys 50, 54, 81–2, 99–100, 111, 145
Bragg, 85
Bronfenbrenner, U. 44, 92, 101
Brown, A.L. and Palincsar, A.S. 141

Browne, A. 52, 169
Bruner, J.S. 89, 105, 121–2, 127, 169
Buhler, K. 60
building a culture 139, 147

caregivers 60
Chen, Y. and Gregory, E. 150–1, 169
Clay, M.M. and Cazden, C.B. 121
co-construction of an idea 126
cognition 15, 37, 127, 167, 170, 172, 173 metacognition 69, 136
cognitive apprenticeships 87; challenge 140, 152
Cole, M. 25, 34, 42, 46, 48–9, 92, 24, 100, 102, 169, 170, 171, 172, 174
collaborative 27, 37, 93, 95
collective 14, 91–5, 100, 164
communication 5, 16–17, 38, 60–1, 64–6, 70, 74–5, 86, 90, 127, 170
communities 12, 18, 29–30, 36, 74, 80, 95, 113, 126, 128, 144, 169, 170, 171, 172, 173, 174
community of practice 4, 16–17, 30, 87–8, 118, 127
compare 4, 17, 24, 35, 38, 41, 49, 65, 77, 109 *see* higher mental functions
compensatory 161, 166
competent child 133, 136, 138; *see also* Reggio Emilia
concepts 6, 13–4, 21, 28, 31–2, 38, 49, 50, 53, **58–88**, 98, 107–10, 113, 119, 125, 131, 140–2, 147, 150, 153, 159, 162–3, 165, 170, 174 everyday 66–7, 70, 80, 83, 88, 140, 150, 163; abstract 38, 67–8, 80, 86, 125, 162; everyday 66–7, 70, 80–3, 88, 140, 150, 163 higher order 4, 16–7, 20, 24, 27–8, 48, 58, 59, 69, 78, 105, 109, 113, 117, 162, 165, 170, 174

pre-concepts 107–8, 119; pseudoconcepts 66, 108–9, 119; scientific 66–71, 80, 83, 86, 88, 107–8, 110, 150, 163, 170, 174
conceptual 30, 42, 67, 92, 174
concrete 12, 19, 27, 79, 86, 90, 102, 106, 108–12, 162
conscious thought 63, 69
consciousness 13, 17, 28, 54, 98, 128, 172
constructivist/socioconstructivist 70, 87
context 20–1, 23, 28, 34, 37, **41–57**, 59, 67, 73, 76, 79–80, 87, 89, 95–6, 114, 146, 150, 154, 161, 167, 170, 173
meaningful 79–80
conversation 3, 47, 109, 134
creativity 115, 133
cultural constructions 12; habitus 8, 18, 30; tools 4, 7, 10, 16, **18–40**, 47–8, 52–9, 64, 70, 71, 75, 78–83, 86, 88, 90, 94–5, 98, 116, 117, 122, 127, 130, 133, 139, 144–6, 148, 151, 154, 159–62, 164
values 11, 139, 144
culturally mediated 5, 32, 66
culture 7, 10–14, **17–29**, 32–8, **41–57**, 67, 75–7, 80, 82, 87–8, 95, 97–8, 100–101, 104, 113–4, 122, 127, 133, 138, 139–40, 144–9, 153, 155, 158–60, 164–7, 170

D'Andrade, R. 41–2, 170
Damon, W. and Phelps, E. 87
Daniels, H. *et al*. 159, 160
Darwin, c. 1
Datta, M. 81, 122, 170
deeply engaging 103, 117
defectology 158, 166, 172
deprivation 159–161
development 1–2, 13–14, 16, 18, 22, 24, 27, 30, 34, 37, 41, 44, 46, 55–6, 59–60, 62, 64, 73, 83, 93–5, 102, 112, 158, 160, 163–4: challenging behaviour 165; concepts 69, 80; cultural 159, 162; emotional 116, 162; everyday concepts 140; higher mental functions 105, 153, 161; intellectual 30, 105, 106, 114, 115, 161; language 71; natural 158–60; motor 161; scientific concepts 110
developmental delay 4, 165; diary 1, 18, 60; niches 44, 56; pedagogy 101
dialectical 13, 18, 98, 163
dialogic 30, 141–2, 155, 169, 174
dialogue 16, 30, 65, 74, 87, 89, 92, 98, 101, 121, 146, 173
didactic 141, 155

discourse 99, 101, 169
discourse guides 96, 101
diversity 92–3, 98, 144, 170
document 86
Donaldson, M. 79, 170
Down's Syndrome 157, 165
drama 140, 148–9, 153–5, 171
Drummond, M.J. 84, 170
Duncan, R.M. and Tarulli, D. 94
Dunn, J. 6
Durant, A. *et al*. 36
Dyson, A.H. 54, 147, 170
Dziurla, R. 109, 170

Early Years Foundation Stage 116
ecological 44–5, 56–7, 94, 101
Elkonin, D. 61, 170
emotions 27, 39, 64
engagement 128, 165, 171
Engeström, Y. 91–3, 171
evidence 85, 101, 125, 133, 147
exile 8, 42–3
exosystem 44–6, 56
expectations 30, 44, 86, 114, 128, 133, 136, 164
experience 19, 25–7, 29–30, 39, 65–7, 70, 74–5, 78, 86, 93, 97, 100.102, 104–5, 112, 130, 133, 140, 152, 161, 167, 169; cultural 80, 82, 145; concrete/first-hand 66, 79, 90, 108, 133, 140, 163; everyday 27, 31, 116; mediated 19, 25–7, 88; prior 75, 80, 86
explicit forms of mediation 75–6
extended families 165
external processes 58
external stimulus 22, 31

family and community 16, 35, 44, 73
family members 61, 74, 160
feedback 121, 124, 133–6, 141
feelings 6, 27, 29, 30, 34, 62, 74, 78, 104–7, 117, 130
Feuerstein *et al* 159, 171
Fifth Dimension 94–5, 102, 169, 170
Figueiredo, M. 83–4
free-flow play 104, 119
Freire, P. 43, 171, 172
functional equivalence 66

games with rules 115
gender 99, 169
generalise 4, 13, 15, 18, 24, 38, 59, 107–8, 159; *see also* higher order mental functions

genetic laws 78–9, 88–9
girls 47, 54, 77, 99–100, 122, 145–6, 151, 157
Goldschmied, E. and Jackson, S. 149, 156, 171
Grainger, T. 149, 169, 171, 173
grammar 42, 58, 63, 72
graphics 35, 152
Gregory, E. 36, 80, 150
Gregory, E. *et al.* 69, 147, 148, 169, 170.171.172.173.174
guided participation 30, 38, 95, 121, 126, 128, 135, 151
Gura, P. 142–3, 171

Hall, Nigel 150, 171, 172
Hamlet 9, 11
Hegel, G. 13–14
historical 16, 21–2, 30, 33, 38, 53, 73, 75, 90, 94, 100, 174
hypothesise 112, 119, 141, 153

identity 30, 36, 38, 55, 93, 99, 159, 171
ideologies 14, 44–5
imitation 5, 16, 18, 60, 65, 163
implicit mediation 76
inclusion 164, 172
independence 38, 79, 117, 137, 140, 172
inner speech
instincts 47
instruction 26, 36, 67, 83–4, 87, 94, 150, 155, 169, 170, 171, 172, 173, 174
interaction 2–6, 10, 13, 16–19, 24–5, 27–9, 35–7, 44–7, 49, 51, 54, 56–7, 59–61, 65–7, 71, 73, 75–6, 78, 80–1, 85, 87–8, 90, 94, 96–8, 101, 104–5, 114–5, 117, 121, 124–5, 127–8, 130, 133, 136–7, 139, 141, 148, 150–1, 154, 159, 161–4, 167–9, 171, 173
interests 17, 28, 93, 103, 112, 116, 125, 128, 133, 140, 147, 152, 163;
intermental 67, 71, 79
internalisation 28, 30, 38, 58, 59, 63, 67, 69, 82, 162, 172
internalise 25, 27, 43, 67, 78, 81, 131, 152
interpsychological 25, 28, 39
intersubjectivity 78, 127, 137
interthinking 95, 101
intramental 67, 71, 79
intrapsychological 25, 28, 39, 121, 137
involuntary responses 47
Isaacs, S. 112–3, 132–3, 171

Jane, B. and Robbin, J. 67
joint collective action 91; mediated activity 95, 102
judgements 74, 160

Karmiloff-Smith, A. 27–8, 171
Kearney, C. 92–3, 171
Kelly, C. 127, 171
Kenner, C. 35, 63, 69, 87, 129–30, 171, 172; and Kress, g. 148, 172
knowledge 1, 2, 14, 16, 21, 29, 30, 35–6, 39, 41, 53, 67, 69, 80–3, 86–7, 95, 104, 125, 127, 130, 137–9, 144, 169, 171, 172
Kozulin, A. 8, 11, 172; and Gindis, B. 163, 172

language: additional 73, 76–7, 98; dominant 90; first 60, 77, 127, 140, 144, 149, 151; home 74; language-play 60; language-rich classroom 98, 150; *see also* cultural tools
languages 7, 9, 35–6, 42, 60–1, 74, 80, 82, 86, 88, 98–9, 101, 123, 140, 144–5, 148, 151, 154
Lanigan, G. 110, 112, 172
Lave, J. and Wenger, E. 81, 95
learning: active 2, 16; collaborative 95; early 1; enhance 166; learning environment 165; learning outcomes/targets 125, 152; learning opportunities 100, 136; learning higher order concepts 98; learning styles 148; learning to 23, 25, 30, 45–6, 86, 127, 140, 147; mediate 127; modes of learning; 140, 153; previous 14; school 40; successful/effective 139, 144, 151
Leontiev, A.N. 10, 14, 90–2, 170, 172
Levi, P. 11, 172
Levina, R. 63
Levine, J. 97–8, 172
listen 4, 76, 81, 84, 86, 96, 115, 127, 131–3, 146
logical thought 66, 71
lower mental process 27
Luria, A.R. 10, 14–5, 31, 48, 75, 90, 170, 172

macrosystem 45–6, 56
make-believe/pretend/imaginative play 40, 94, 96, 105, 108, 112–7, 119, 132, 143, 147, 149, 153
Malaguzzi, L. 154, 172
Marxism 9
material tool 49, 57

mathematics 22, 40, 53, 86, 128, 162, 169
Matusov, E. 30, 172
meaning-makers 52, 174
mediation 12, 16, 19, **21–39**, 52–3, 70, 75–6, 78, 82, 86, 89–91, 95, 122, 148, 161, 163–4, 174
memory 10, **21–39**, 49, 58–9, 65–6, 76–9, 82–3, 107, 115, 117, 131, 161, 171
mesosystem 44–5, 57, 114
metalinguistic 130
microsystem 44–5, 57
mnemonic devices 23–4, 31–4, 39, 75
model/modelling 7, 11, 19, 30, 44–5, 78, 80–1, 87, 100, 124, 127, 130, 134–5, 140–2, 152; role 10, 30, 93, 124
Moll, I.C. 86, 170, 172
monologue 63–4, 71, 134
more expert other 25–6, 39, 54, 76, 78, 85, 89, 94, 101, 121, 126, 129–31, 136, 138, 140, 143
movement (and senses) 59, 80, 104
music 3, 7, 18, 22, 30, 34, 40, 42, 46, 53–4, 71, 75–6, 106, 128, 140, 146, 154–5, 168; *see also* cultural tools

needs of children 77, 158, 163–5
negotiation 13, 86, 92, 95, 122–4, 136, 138, 147, 153
neighbourhood 44–5, 95, 102, 164
Newman, D. *et al.* 86, 172
numbers 28, 31, 33, 69, 84, 130, 162
numerical systems 35
Nurse, A. 165, 172

objectification 12, 14, 19
object-orientated 62
objects 3, 12, 14, 17–8, 25, 28, 31, 33–4, 36–7, 39–40, 42, 52–3, 58–9, 68–70, 77–8, 80–1, 84–5, 90, 104–11, 114, 116–7, 148–50, 153, 156, 162
observation 1, 3, 6, 18, 67, 81, 84–6, 99, 110, 112–15, 123–4, 131, 145, 151
one to one correspondence 33, 122
ownership 31, 121, 128

Paley, V.G. 95–6, 172
participation 30, 37, 39, 78, 81–2, 95
partnerships 74–5, 98, 101, 151
patterns 2, 5, 115, 129, 151
Pea, R.D. 33–4, 173
pedagogy 10, 25, 66, 70, 75, 83, 98, 101, 124, 133, 137, 139–40, 170, 172, 173

peer teaching 16, 35, 82, 121, 129–30, 143, 150
peers 29, 35, 44, 63, 76, 80, 87, 139, 147, 154, 157–60, 163, 167, 169, 170, 171, 172, 173
performance level 85
physical 4, 13, 19, 21, 32–3, 41, cues 58; difficulties 154–66; exploration 85; needs 24, 154; play 153 properties 66; props or objects 107, tools 122, 145; world 47, 104
Piaget, J. 59–60, 64, 70–1, 94, 169
planning 18, 98, 140–1, 149–53, 162, 173
play: and meaning **100–19**; blockplay **65–6**, 106, 125, 130–1, 142, 143, 167, 171; role 114–17, 143; solitary play 103–4, 117; with objects 116; with rules 95, 105, 113; *see also* make-believe
potential 44, 66, 85, 91, 117, 122, 127
power 9, 12, 22, 51, 53, 167
practices 11, 14, 28, 30, 35, 37, 42, 56, 114, 116, 118, 144, 173
practise 61, 151
Pramling, N. and Samuelson, I.P. 110
predict 4–5, 20, 22
pre-verbal thought 61
problem-solving 24, 33, 64–5, 83, 96, 151
psychobiological 27, 39
purpose 12, 31, 65, 80, 98, 108, 127, 134, 153

questioning 77, 80, 110, 121, 131, 133, 139, 140, 148, 149

reading 3, 8, 10, 19, 21, 23, 40, 42, 53, 56, 106, 128, 141, 162; shared 122–3, 137
reared 44, 151
recall 4, 14, 20, 39; *see also* memory
reciprocal teaching 87, 89, 129–30, 141, 172
referential 62, 71
reflect on 7, 31, 58, 64, 67, 69–70, 82, 95, 98, 131, 134, 136–7, 154
Reggio Emilia 13, 47, 74, 133, 137–8, 148, 165, 169, 172, 173
rehearse *see* practise 65
relationship 31, 47, 52, 62, 108, 163
religions 29, 45
remember 20, 23–4, 27–31, 58, 78, 133; *see also* memory, recall
represent 22–3, 33–4, 40, 49, 53, 93, 106–8, 116, 119–20, 140–1, 154
respect 9, 10, 98, 139, 144–5, 151, 165, 168; respectful relationships 74

Rinaldi, C. 74, 131, 133, 173
risk-free 103, 116; *see also* play
Rogoff, B. 30, 38, 95, 126–7, 136, 171, 173, 174
role of adults 135
role play 114–7, 143; *see also* play
Romero, M.E. 80–1, 173
routines of the day 47, 57, 154
rule-bound 6, 20, 95, 140
rules 5, 20, 30, 43, 58, 72, 79, 91–5, 98, 105–6, 113–7, 128, 140, 150, 153

Sacharov, Lev 65
Sachs, Albie 43
Saussure, F. de 52, 173
scaffolding 85–9, 117, 121–5, 133, 136–7, 140, 151, 164, 170
science 67, 86
scientific concepts *see* concepts
Scribner, S. 43, 173
self-chosen 103, 116, 119; *see also* play
semiotics 40, 52, 57, 167, 170
senses 2, 59, 80, 104, 131, 132, 153, 160
sequence 35, 37, 41, 95, 122, 129, 137
sharing 22, 28, 37, 38, 60, 71, 81–2, 87, 125, 127, 140, 148, 151; sharing attention 90, 98, 134
siblings 16, 29, 36, 44–5, 74, 80, 81, 161, 169, 170, 171, 172, 173
significant moment 9, 106
signs 7, 11, 18, 22–3, 28, 33, 40, 52–61, 71, 75–6, 78, 90, 91, 104–7, 117, 128, 150, 163
sign-users 128
simultaneous worlds 148, 156
situated learning 87, 89, 172
Smith, Mary 97, 173
social world 3, 16, 20, 54, 75, 80, 99, 113
socialisation 37, 47, 80–1
sociohistorical 7, 20, 73, 75, 150, 158, 167, 170, 172
solitary play *see* play
special needs 10, 16, 154, 158–66, 172
speech **58–79**, 134; acommunicative 65, 70; egocentric 60, 65–5, 71 (*see also* monologues); inner 58, 60, 63–4, 69, 75, 78–9, 134; social 69
spontaneous concepts *see* everyday concepts, under concepts
stereotypes 74
sustained shared thinking 121–7, 138

symbolic 31, 34, 40, 53, 56–7, 64, 153; function 106, 120; play 116; system 59, 69, 95, 106, 128, 140, 149, 154, 163; tools 40, 64, 91, 134, 159
symbols 7, 18, 22–4, 28, 33–5, 40, 52–60, 71, 75, 84, 104–8, 117, 119, 128, 140, 150, 153

targets 116, 152, 153
teaching 9–10, 16, 25, 35–6, 66, 69, **70–89**, 98, 100, 108, 124, 130, 133, 136–7, **139–51**, 155, 163–4, 167; dialogic 30, 141–2, 155, 169, 174; peer 16, 35, 82, 121, 129–30, 143, 150; reciprocal 16, 35, 82, 121, 129–30, 143, 150 strategy 137; *see also* pedagogy
technology 67, 86, 127, 157, 163, 171
theories 2, 59, 80, 86, 104, 112, 121, 131, 133–5, 153
theory of mind 130
thinking 5, 10, 16, 18, 22–4, 33–7, 41, 49, 53, **58–71**, 74, 78–9, 84, 89–90, 95, 98, 101, 104, 109, 113, 135–6, 138, 142, 145, 149, 171; abstract 27, 102, 119–20, 153; complex 6; everyday 27; higher order 109, 118, 120; logical 13, 6-; naïve 133; primitive 15; refining 33; shared 121, 124–5, 127, 138; skills 142, 173; verbal 27, 64, 105–6
thought 17, 23, 41, **58–69**, 71, 78, 83, 104, 107; conscious 63, 69; independent 135; logical 66, 71; pre-verbal 61; problem-solving 64; thought processes 14
transformation 31, 147
transition 14, 27, 31, 60, 71, 78–9, 89, 94, 108, 119
transmission of culture 122, 138

values 19, 29, 37, 41–3, 46, 51, 55, 75, 86–8, 98, 138–9, 144
voluntary control 67–8, 72
Vygodskaya, G. 7–8, 173

Wells, G. 30, 52, 67, 127
world of culture 13–14
writing 22–3, 33–5, 40, 53, 75, 106, 123–4, 128–30, 147, 150, 152, 154

zone of proximal development 71, 89, 94, 116–7, 121, 140, 163, 170, 174

eBooks

eBooks – at www.eBookstore.tandf.co.uk

A library at your fingertips!

eBooks are electronic versions of printed books. You can store them on your PC/laptop or browse them online.

They have advantages for anyone needing rapid access to a wide variety of published, copyright information.

eBooks can help your research by enabling you to bookmark chapters, annotate text and use instant searches to find specific words or phrases. Several eBook files would fit on even a small laptop or PDA.

NEW: Save money by eSubscribing: cheap, online access to any eBook for as long as you need it.

Annual subscription packages

We now offer special low-cost bulk subscriptions to packages of eBooks in certain subject areas. These are available to libraries or to individuals.

For more information please contact webmaster.ebooks@tandf.co.uk

We're continually developing the eBook concept, so keep up to date by visiting the website.

www.eBookstore.tandf.co.uk